12 book

CW01090961

HTeBooks

Disclaimer

This book is designed to provide condensed information. It is not intended to reprint all the information that is otherwise available, but instead to complement, amplify and supplement other texts. You are urged to read all the available material, learn as much as possible and tailor the information to your individual needs.

Every effort has been made to make this book as complete and as accurate as possible. However, there may be mistakes, both typographical and in content. Therefore, this text should be used only as a general guide and not as the ultimate source of information. The purpose of this book is to educate.

The author or the publisher shall have neither liability nor responsibility to any person or entity with respect to any loss or damage caused, or alleged to have been caused, directly or indirectly, by the information contained in this book.

Table of Contents

How To Apply The Teachings Of Buddhism In The 21st Century

Why Buddhism, you may ask? Buddhism provides you with a complete set of proven practices that lead you to live a fulfilling life. The basis of Buddhism is drawn from a human perspective and ability. You carry your own destiny. While some religions believe the need to have a supreme being and to worship this Supreme Being, Buddhism does not have any supreme being but rather your goal is to continually be enlightened and live a happier, stress free life in this very hectic world.

This book will help you understand more about Buddhism, the benefits of Buddhism as well as how you can practice Buddhism in the 21st Century. Additionally, since Buddhism emphasizes so much in the mind, you will also learn how you can exploit the tremendous power within your own mind.

Why Buddhism

"We are shaped by our thoughts; we become what we think. When the mind is pure, joy follows like a shadow that never leaves."

- Buddha

Before we can even start practicing Buddhism, it is critical that we understand why choose Buddhism in the first place. The amazing thing about Buddhism is that it focuses more on the mind and the role the mind plays in transforming every sphere of your life of course including your wrongdoing. Therefore, if the mind is transformed, does any wrong doing remain? Of course not. This is among the many benefits of Buddhism. Let us have a look at the different ways that you can benefit from adopting Buddhism.

Buddhism is an Age Old Practice

Buddhism is an age-old practice that dates to over 2500 years since its inception and has been tried and tested. There is a hot debate as to whether Buddhism should really be called a religion. Indeed, by western standards, Buddhism is unique. It contains teachings that focus on humanity. The latter is the reason why it is often described as a man centered religion.

Buddhism was made popular by Gautama Buddha after he became enlightened. The nature of Buddhist practice is anchored in a philosophy that seeks to attain the highest level of human performance and existence through exploring the mind. Buddhism believes that there is an inseparable link between the living things. It also emphasizes on understanding the continuous flow of nature. The world is not static. One living being transforms into another and recurs to live another cycle. Thus, life is cyclic.

It is an Adoptive Philosophy

Modern Buddhism or Buddhism in the 21st C is adoptive and evolving. The basic tenets of Buddhist practice reflect a lot more relevance to you now than ever before. The need for you to practice Buddhism is ever more increasing and urgent, if you intend to lead a happy life with peace of mind.

The world in the 21st century is in constant turmoil. This turmoil exerts pressure on individuals. Sometimes it is not possible for you to bear the pressure anymore. Buddhism meets you at this point of desperation. Unlike other religions, Buddhism lays the possibility of restoration of peace, joy and calm in your hands. You are guided through the various sutras and philosophies of Buddhism until you recapture the ever more illusive ideal of eternal happiness, peace and calm. Yes, Buddhism challenges you to explore the power within your own mind to harvest what you so yearn for.

Buddhism is compatible with your Ideals and Science

Modern Buddhism appeals to your modern ideals and scientific facts. Scientists have cited elements of Buddhism as true reflections of scientific fact. Many other elements are yet to be fully understood by science. They are not disputed either. Application of some Buddhist tools to resolve issues of human health is in common practice. One such tool is the use of meditation to manage some medical conditions such as cancer and asthma. There is, therefore proof that Buddhism has always been right about the power of the mind to grant you control over the physical developments and emotional dynamics.

Buddhism is in Harmony with the Environment

The environment is at threat because of the lack of understanding of the laws of nature by man. Man's desires and insatiable greed has caused destruction upon the very structures that he seeks to lean on for survival. By learning the truths explained in Buddhist practice, you learn how to avoid the persuasions of the flesh and excesses that are reminiscent of human nature. Buddhism also fosters a peaceful coexistence with those around you. You naturally begin to see more good in others. They also reciprocate because you have become friendlier and easy to be around. Buddhism ensures that you live in harmony with both human and non-human environment enhancing harmony with the environment.

Buddhism Is Nonjudgmental

One of the reasons why you stand to grow and achieve your dreams in Buddhism today is because it is one of the few religions that do not castigate you. Buddhism is a comfortable home to all. It does not consider other religions as good or bad. It is a complete set that does not need to brainwash you. Furthermore, Buddhism is your only chance to get meaningful answers to questions you have about life. It is only through learning and applying the principles of Buddhism that you gain access to eternal and irrefutable truths. It presents you with complete teachings that do not make reference to the mysterious world. Buddhism presents you with a real opportunity to witness positive change. Therefore, Buddhism is an open door for you irrespective of what religion you subscribe to.

It is Accessible

You need a religion that is available whenever you need it. You do not need intermediaries in Buddhism. Once you have mastered the teachings and the fundamentals, you can practice Buddhism on your own. It is a religion that is meant to be part of your daily life.

Buddhism has also evolved and has provided for creative and progressive means to enable people access it. You can walk into a Buddhist learning center in your locality and start off. It also does not come with strings attached. Additionally, Buddhism is a free for all religion, a practice that is inspired by the ultimate goal of the originator, Gautama Buddha, that people deserve to be enlightened.

As mentioned earlier, you can also learn Buddhism through unconventional means such as the internet. You will find many platforms that provide free lessons for those willing to join Buddhism on the internet.

*Key point/action step

As they say, you can only know how sweet the honey is by tasting. The only way you can truly know the benefits of Buddhism is by adopting the practice and seeing how you can benefit from it.

How to Practice Buddhism in the 21st Century

"If by leaving a small pleasure one sees a great pleasure, let a wise person leave the small pleasure and look to the great."

- Dhammapada 290 / Müller & Maguire, 2002.

Now that you know how you can benefit from Buddhism, let's see how you can practice Buddhism. The practice of Buddhism in modern day is not completely different from the classic practice but only different in various respects. This difference is both inevitable and necessary if the practice is to remain relevant to the modern person. Modern Buddhism still borrows the fundamental tenets from classic practice. These principles are molded and adjusted to fit life in the 21st century. The establishment of learning centers is an example of a shift from the classic way in which Buddhism was dispensed to those who wished to subscribe to its ideals.

Accessing Buddhism

Access to Buddhism teachings has been made easier by availing the full content of the philosophy on the internet. This is a more liberal approach to Buddhism. Yet it does not violate any of the Buddhism fundamentals. In fact, the practice of Buddhism in the 21st century has bolstered one of the main drivers of the concept of Buddhism; that the world is in a continuous state of change. Embracing change is core to the practice of Buddhism. You can now learn all you need about Buddhism from your nearest Buddhism learning center. The cost of building temples has been eliminated, thus making Buddhism more accessible to you.

You can also learn Buddhism on your own. There are authentic websites dedicated to the teaching of Buddhism. This makes it easier to incorporate Buddhism into your lifestyle and discover the benefits without feeling as though it is eating up the already shrinking little time you can afford each day.

Focus On Enriching Your Mind

In a world full of chaos and restlessness, you need a religion that teaches you how to discipline your mind so you don't lose it. Buddhism is anchored on exploring the power of your mind. You can only gain control of yourself if you explore the possibilities and the power your mind exerts on everything else around you.

This ultimate control is gained through following the systematic teachings as provided in the four noble truths. The noble truths culminate into the eight fold path. The latter is believed to be the peak of Buddhism practice.

The Four Noble Truths

The truth of dukkha (suffering)

The first truth focuses on realizing life's challenges. It is referred to as the truth of dukkha. We live in a world that keeps presenting us with a myriad of challenges. You definitely need a solution to these ever emerging and ever evolving challenges. Through teaching on the essence of dukkha, you learn that the world is in a continuous state of change. Once you embrace change, you ride the tide. You are not swept by the tide. You also gain an inner understanding of how the world works. This truth prepares you for such life realities and challenges such as pain, illness, suffering, disappointments, anxiety, and stress. If Buddhism can equip you with skills to handle the mentioned life encounters, then you are in for a treat of your life in the 21st C. Several of these challenges appear on just about everyone's list of life concerns in modern day. Many of these people have no clue of how to get rid of or get over the concerns. Only Buddhism has a well devised set of instruction that successfully resolve these dilemmas.

The truth of the arising or cause of dukkha

The second truth is learning the origin of your problems and staying proactive at dealing with them (the truth of the origin of dukkha). If there is a necessary tool in the effort to prepare against the unknown, then it is knowing where your problem comes from. In a world full of challenges, each of us has a list of challenges, which keep occurring, yet we do nothing about them. We do nothing because we do not know how. We do not know because we have not embraced Buddhism. This second truth emphasizes on knowledge. The body of knowledge is obviously larger than it was a few years back. Each year comes with a new development, which is typically how nature should be. Yet, we need to understand the nature and origin of the changes to prepare ourselves for possible turns. Buddhism encourages you to shun ignorance and gain insight to the recall the causes of the problems that come your way.

Usually, the cause of suffering is usually because of our need to desire for more. It is understandable if you are one of those faced with a constant need to amass more than you really need. It is still understandable that you succumb to the cravings of the flesh such as desire to engage in immoral sexual acts. It is only a normal human weakness. It is also likely that you abhor some of the things you do because of succumbing to the demands of the flesh. If this applies to you, then you need to take time to learn the nature and origin of the temptations as well as suffering. Once you understand that your own body takes you captive, you can use the power of your mind to resist and prevent the onset of the acts of dukkha as described by the teachings of this truth.

The Truth of the Cessation of the Arising Dukkha

Now that you have known the source and cause of your problems in life, it is high time you learnt how to effectively cut links with these causes. You must take an active role in stopping the causes of suffering in your life. Buddhism leads you on a mental path that seeks to permanently cut all links that may be the cause of your suffering.

The Truth of the Path Leading To the Cessation Of Dukkha

This is the fourth truth that is taught as a chore element of understanding and practicing Buddhism. This truth is one that opens out into the eight fold path meant to lead you to the ultimate understanding of life and attainment of nirvana. If Buddhism provides you with an opportunity to systematically rise to a state of purity where dukkha does not exist then you have a safe haven. Yes, a safe haven from your current state of restlessness, ignorance of the noble truths and the danger of despair.

The eightfold path

Right Understanding: Understand that the Four noble truths are true and noble.

Right thought: Having the emotional intelligence to act in love and compassion as well as having a mind able to let go.

Right Speech: Uplifting, truthful and non-harmful communication. This means that you need to avoid lying, slander and gossip among other kinds of harmful communication.

Right Action: You need to avoid exploitation of others and self. This means that you need to follow the five precepts of Buddhism as indicated below:

*Do not kill or cause harm to other living beings

*Abstain from drugs and alcohol that cloud your mind

*Avoid false speech

*Avoid sexual misconduct

*Do not steal

Right Livelihood: Earning a livelihood that does not violate self and others.

Right Effort: You need to consciously direct your life energy into transformation for the better. This means avoiding negative thoughts that generate negative energy like jealousy and anger.

Right Mindfulness: You need to have a clear sense of your mental as well as body health.

Right Concentration: Samadhi mean to be absorbed fixed or established at one point. This means that you need to teach your mind to focus on one object to achieve a sense of calmness, which can only be achieved through meditation. Achieving the highest sense of concentration leads to enlightenment.

The objective of Buddhism is to enlighten you. Once you are enlightened, you become a better person, a productive person, and a knowledgeable person who adds value to human existence. Yet, enlightenment is a mere objective for all who practice Buddhism. It is the highest level of mind power and awareness. A few people have managed to achieve this feat. It is difficult to describe what you enjoy at this point since the uplifting of your power rises above simple human descriptions.

*Key point/action step

As we have seen from this chapter, Buddhism concentrates on the power of the mind. I cannot emphasize further the importance of the mind in Buddhism. By adopting the noble truths and the eightfold path that leads to enlightenment, the mind plays an important role in all these.

Buddhism In Practice

"Realization is not knowledge about the universe, but the living experience of the nature of the universe. Until we have such living experience, we remain dependent on examples, and subject to their limits."

Chogyal Namkhai Norbu, from "The Crystal and the Way of Light"

So, now that you have known the benefits of Buddhism, how can you use it in your day to day life?

Use Buddhism to provide answers to your Dilemmas

If you come from a religious setting in which you have more questions than answers about what you preach or profess, then you have come to the home of answers. The concept of a supreme being can be a challenge to understand. It is a dilemma to many people who subscribe to God centered religions. You may be left with many unanswered questions about the supernatural being you serve. Therefore, you may feel a disconnection between your physical being and the ideal person you would wish to be. The reason here being that you are only human and cannot achieve acts linked with the supernatural. Buddhism, thus, provides you with practical answers. You do not have to ponder about whether you can be your best or not. The achievement of your objectives now entirely depends on you. It is not in the control of any other power but you.

Use Buddhism to enact Positive Change

The mentioned state of chaos of the world today would not occur in the first place if world citizens practiced Buddhism with total commitment. Yet, this is a feat that is achievable. Accomplishment of great matters often starts with one person. That person is you. Can you be part of a solution to so much distress, suffering and pain people experience around the world? Buddhism helps you understand that the power to change for the better lies in your mind and nowhere else.

Use Buddhism to get a sense of Peace and Mental Calm

I'm sure that your heart warms up when I mention such ideals as calm, peace, happiness and calm. Indeed, we all yearn for these ideals. However, it is true that many people have found happiness and calmness an elusive experience. The amazing thing is that Buddhism seeks to resolve many issues that face your consciousness. Many of the issues your mind attempts to resolve do not have solutions. The consequent effect is anxiety and stress. Buddhism applies proven tools such as meditation to tame your monkey mind and restore calmness. It is not possible to view life objectively with a restless mind.

The practice of such meditation techniques as mindfulness provides a practical approach, and result oriented step to resolving your anxieties, unease, stresses, and strains.

Use Buddhism to Achieve Self Awareness

We are constantly trying to understand why things happen the way they do. We seek to understand why people act the way they do. However, many of these attempts are in vain because we do not start with understanding ourselves. Self-awareness is critical to gaining insightful lessons on how the world works. You have probably heard that animals sense devastating natural catastrophes coming well in advance. Such animals then proceed to migrate to safety. The incidence of tsunamis and the emergence of hurricanes have elicited such reactions from animals.

Human beings have for many years alluded to the existence of the sixth sense. Indeed, human beings have inherent ability to sense such occurrences. A few people have been reported as having foretold forthcoming events such as imminent floods and even explosions. Closer home, you have probably thought of making a call to someone you have not contacted for long, and before your thought winds up, you receive a call from the same person. Such sensation is reminiscent of the sporadic flashes of the power your mind. You do not always enjoy this extra-ordinary experience because your mind is held captive to the constant prompts and never-ending crisis that is the hallmark of the world we live in today. Buddhism helps you release your mind from the captivity of crisis so that you can have some self-awareness, which can also help you know how the world around you is likely to be and behave.

Use Buddhism for better Health

Buddhism has inherent practices that enable you to enjoy bliss of health. Modern medicine and other science research has established that the mind is a source of many problems that afflict humanity. In modern medicine, medical conditions such as asthma, high blood pressure, and even cancer have been managed through the application of such Buddhist practices as meditation. In addition, modern medicine has demonstrated that through the practice of calming the mind, which is the main goal of Buddhism, the human brain is able to generate certain substances, which improve your ability to resist infections. In other words, the practice of Buddhism and meditation in particular, will help you improve your immune system.

Use Buddhism to get control of your life

You need control to handle life. Once you embrace the systematic teachings of Buddhism such as the four noble truths and become aware of the five precepts, you gain control of your emotions and other physical influences of life. This is an important precursor to your successful handling of the stresses and strains of life. Once you become enlightened, you accept the inevitable course of nature, avoid challenges you can proactively avert and stay calm and peaceful irrespective of the circumstances prevailing.

Use Buddhism to help you understand the Continuity of Human Life

The knowledge that life is a continuous cycle enables you to understand the inevitable. Such life experiences as death no longer rock you out of your mind. You accept it with calmness and the wisdom that emanates from enlightenment. It is an irony that death has been around for as long as man has existed but it still catches many people unawares. The reaction to such a phenomenon should have been one of acceptance and calmness, but alas, it is a cause for acrimony, and disheartenments for those outside the realms of Buddhism. Buddhism is therefore your rational and realistic panacea to most of the experiences that deprive you control. Once you understand that nothing is detached in its existence, you embrace the world as it is and fit in the overall plan without acrimony.

*Key point/action step

As you can see, you can use Buddhism in every aspect of your life. It is basically an answer to all the questions you have. And the answers don't lie in some foreign power but in you.

How to Deal With Pain and Suffering

"All that we are is the result of what we have thought. It is founded on our thoughts. It is made up of our thoughts. If one speaks or acts with an evil thought, pain follows one, as the wheel follows the foot of the ox that draws the wagon"

-Dhammapada 1-2 / Müller & Maguire, 2002.

One would expect that since the world has advanced in technology, the physical suffering that those who came before us encountered is no longer applicable to us. Ironically though, pain and suffering appears to have increased in intensity and frequency in modern day. Buddhism has you covered in dealing with the pain and suffering that has become so prevalent in modern day.

The first stop at your marvel with the dilemmas caused by suffering is the understanding of the root cause of suffering as exemplified in the four noble truths. Buddhism helps you in understanding and internalizing the essence of the dharma (the teachings of Buddha) on wisdom and compassion. Buddhism does not evade the facts.

Origins of Your Suffering

Through the teachings, Buddha acknowledges that pain and suffering are part of the cycle of life and death. It is further explained that suffering is a result of either a past or present karma. Thus, Buddhism acknowledges the existence of suffering as inevitable. Yet, although that does not sound like good news, wait and listen to the conclusions as proclaimed by dharma (the teachings of Buddhism for life).

By following the teachings and applying them, you begin to detach yourself from the prison of physical suffering. Although dharma teaches that all sentient beings are prone to suffering, there is still a solution to pain and suffering. This solution is embodied in the dharma. In simple terms, we need to appreciate the fact that life is full of suffering/dissatisfaction.

Types of Suffering

The Buddhist philosophy classifies human suffering into two broad categories:

-Suffering of the physical body like death, illness, disappointments, frustrations, and even lack of money

-Suffering of the mind

Owing to reasons already mentioned earlier, the occurrence of the suffering of the human mind is more prevalent than ever. There is a strong co-relation between the suffering of the physical body and suffering of the mind. In most instances, the occurrence of one leads to another. Modern science acknowledges that many health concerns emanate from a poor state of the mind. Buddhism, as you may be aware right now focuses a lot on your mind.

On the other hand, the suffering of the physical body can lead to the suffering of the mind. When you eliminate the suffering of the mind, the physical body is on the path to healing and reprieve. Ironically though, the elimination of the physical suffering does not always lead to a better feeling mentally. Therefore, it means that the mind is of critical importance when it comes to the practice of Buddhism.

Dharma (teachings of Buddha) leads you to a point of fearlessness and mental acceptance. If you follow the teachings, you get to a point of cessation of sadness, defilements, anxiety, and suffering. All these are only possible if you can learn to accept the pattern as an ordained pattern that you must remain as such.

Moreover, Buddhist dharma helps you to understand the principle of cause and effect in a more practical way. The occurrence of Karma now does not always mean immediate repercussion. There is no clear calendar as to when the karma will have to be paid for and by whom. One thing remains constant; the law of cause and effect.

The essence of the various teachings on dealing with pain and suffering can be captured by following the steps below:

*Avoid being deluded by the present state of pain and/or suffering. It is such delusion that leads to mental pain and suffering.

*Repent the past karma and start on a clean slate.

*Engage in constant meditation and contemplation of the nature of life. Buddha is known to have been in a constant state of thought. It is believed that it is such thought and contemplation that led him to unveil the truth that illuminates the world of followers of Buddha.

*Ensure you practice dharma consistently and persistently. Your pain and suffering is the ailment, dharma is your prescription. You can only get to heal if you stick to the prescription. Variations in applying the dharma lead to various in the final result.

*Key point/action step

The ultimate panacea to your suffering and pain is embodied in the dharma. You must follow the teachings and apply them if you expect the healing anticipated in Buddhism.

Buddhism for Success in Business

"A jug fills dropby drop"

- Buddha

Although you may find it difficult to relate the concept of material gain with dharma, you will agree that business activities are part of the cycle widely mentioned in the practice and application of Buddhism. Business today relies heavily on many teachings that Buddhism offers. It is not uncommon to see how modern corporate executives try to apply some Buddhist practices in their lives to try to harvest the most out of their intellectual and physical endowment. Business executives commonly practice meditation and the practice of yoga with an aim to improve their performance.

Yet, the occurrences above may not always be within the scope and practice of Buddhism. The clear truth is that Buddhism encourages you to embrace the flow of nature. It asks you to accept the inevitable situations that may not be pleasant. It also requires you to become proactive about impending problems, which you can avert. Being proactive means doing something that will forestall any encounters that produce pain and suffering. Improving your business through unleashing the power of your mind and that of your staff is a practical application of Buddhist practices in your business.

Getting returns from business can thus be used to prevent certain aspects of pain and suffering. Success, in business, means being able to cater for the physical needs of those who rely on you for such provision. These acts will subsequently smother the effect of lack on the minds of the beneficiaries of the returns from business success.

The most direct application of Buddhist practices in seeking success in business emerges from the eight fold paths. There are three main aspects of the eight fold paths that relate directly to business and provide guidance on how to attain success without succumbing to the desires of the flesh and greed. Let us see these aspects.

Mindfulness

Mindfulness in Buddhism emphasizes the need to focus on the present moment. Any good businessperson must stay aware of what is happening in business at the present moment. Applying mindfulness enables you to focus on what works for your business in the present moment.

Right Intention

Suspicion reins supreme in the modern business circles. Companies are constantly afraid of losing their best employees. They are also in constant fear of the unknown. They grapple with the possibility of their competitors eating into or even eating up their share of the market. Operating from the angle of right intention, can assist you stay calm in business and win many people's trust. The success of a business is widely determined by how large your network is.

The Right Action

Engaging the right action in business cannot be questioned. When you learn to apply this path in your business, you satisfy your customers' needs. You will be keen on giving them value for their money.

The right action also directs you to developing the ultimate code of ethics that helps you and your staff live and work in harmony

*Key point/action step

Embrace professionalism and honesty in your business today. Buddhism is your insurance to success.

How to Apply What You've Learned?

Buddhism in modern day is more of a lifestyle than a religion. If you want to get the most out of the teachings laid out in Buddhism, you must learn to live by the Buddhist ideals every day. Once you have learnt such principles as love, compassion, and self-awareness, try to apply these principles consciously in your daily activities. It is common to encounter challenges that push you to succumb to emotional strain. However, use such moments as opportunities to spread your love and compassion.

Join Buddhism now

Just like the eight fold path proclaims the right intention and the right actions, you will never really enjoy the treasures of Buddhism from the periphery. If you intend to lead a life of fulfillment and calm, you must begin to practice Buddhism. Get yourself an instructor who will guide you through the practice Buddhism. Rise up to the occasion and live like a true Buddhist.

Read More Learn More

It is a Buddhist ideal to ensure that you stay knowledgeable. It is through reading that you explore the depths and the inner truths that the teachings present. There are teachings that go to detail to explain such concepts as the existence of karma, rebirth and how to navigate through the labyrinth that is life by applying the four noble truths.

Share Your Experience by Example

You do not need to tell the world by word of mouth that you are now following the teachings of Buddha, and that you subscribe to Buddhism. Historical records show that Buddhism has largely gained such great following by example. It is non-confrontational but very practical. People volunteer to join to enjoy the peace they witness. Live and act the lessons you learn from the dharma. The calmness, the compassion, and the love you demonstrate can never go unnoticed. Then you achieve a chore principle of Buddhism, which fosters sharing love and shining light for others to see.

How To Control Your Emotions

This book is about emotional intelligence and how to use emotions to solve problems and achieve goals.

You will learn the following in this book:

*The components of emotional intelligence

*What emotions are and what they are for

*How to correctly evaluate what you're feeling

*How to calm yourself down and weaken the effect of powerful emotions

*How to process emotions for you to understand and manage them better

*How to use emotions for motivating yourself to set and get goals despite setbacks

*How to communicate and interact with others using emotional intelligence

Emotional Intelligence

"Emotional intelligence refers to the capacity for recognizing our own feelings and those of others, for motivating ourselves, and for managing emotions well in ourselves and our relationships."

- Daniel Goleman

Emotional intelligence is the ability to recognize emotions (in ourselves and other people) and to manage them well. This includes the following factors:

Self-awareness: Knowing and understanding the emotions that are currently taking place

Self-regulation: Handling emotions in a way that makes them become helpful instead of detrimental to the chosen task, including delaying gratification in favor of pursuing goals and recovering from stress

Motivation: Using emotions to guide actions towards goal fulfillment despite setbacks and difficulty of initiating first actions

Empathy: Perceiving other people's emotions, looking at things from their point of view, and developing rapport with others

Social skills: Dealing with individuals' sentiments in beneficial ways and in the spirit of teamwork

The Importance of Emotional Intelligence

Emotions are tied to a person's thoughts, physical status, and behavior. Because of this, comprehending emotions and managing them effectively provides several benefits:

Improved mental health. Emotions affect how a person thinks and views things. By being intelligent about emotions, thoughts and perspectives become balanced and realistic. It prevents the person from being swept by unpleasant emotions and allows him or her to have a happier life.

Healthier body. Being emotionally intelligent includes knowing how to contend with stressful events. Chronic stress harms the body by weakening it and making it more prone to acquiring illnesses. Since powerful negative feelings contribute to a person's stress, emotional intelligence can greatly improve a person's health by allowing the person to choose empowering feelings instead of stressful ones.

Better relationships. Understanding and controlling one's own emotions allow him or her to relate well with others because feelings can be expressed appropriately and adjusted for the sake of relationships. Comprehending others' sentiments fosters caring and sympathy, which result into more satisfying relationships.

Leadership potential. Leading people requires understanding how they feel about things – it's hard to manage people if you don't know what goes on in their minds. Knowing what they are concerned about allows the leader to do something about them, and when he does, they will be more willing to help with the leader's cause. Emotional intelligence is an important leadership skill because it enables the leader to guide people's emotions, which directs their actions.

Conflict management. Discerning other people's emotions and perspectives can help resolve conflicts and prevent them from happening. Considering the needs and preferences of the people involved makes negotiations easier.

Higher chances of success. A well developed emotional intelligence helps with controlling impulses and gaining motivation to focus on goals. The ability to control what one feels builds self-confidence and perseverance. It leads to building beneficial relationships with other people who can help with the person's objectives. All these contribute to the person's success.

*Emotional intelligence, or the ability to discern and manage emotions, makes us contend better with life. Being emotionally intelligent includes being self-aware, handling your emotions well, being motivated to pursue goals, having empathy towards others, and developing good social skills.

A Primer on Emotions

"Our emotions need to be as educated as our intellect. It is important to know how to feel, how to respond, and how to let life in so that it can touch you."

- Jim Rohn

Emotions are feelings that are composed of physical sensations and thoughts. Psychologists are not certain whether biological responses result into the awareness of emotion or the other way around, but it's generally agreed that emotion has both a mental and physical component. Simply put, emotions are nothing more but felt sensations and a thought about what's being felt. As a result, you can feel the same things – for example, a racing heart and tense muscles – but if you have different thoughts about it, you will also have different emotions (fear if you thought you're in danger and excitement if you are waiting for something good to happen). So, one of the ways to control emotions is relabeling them, which we will discuss later.

Purpose of Emotions

Humans have evolved with emotions because they are useful for us. If they are 100% harmful, our emotional ancestors would have been wiped out before they had a chance to reproduce. Emotions are with us because they are generally geared for our survival and it helps us solve our problems:

It provides valuable information, such as evaluations of the environment and your inner state

It gives you the power and motive to respond to things

Take note that emotions developed when life was relatively simpler than what it is now. Inherently, ancient humans were concerned with surviving harsh prehistoric conditions. Today, we have to deal with extra factors such as conforming to societal rules, considering other people's feelings, protecting our self-image, and working for long-term goals. Unfortunately, our emotions are built for prehistoric conditions and they have changed very little over the thousands of years. That's why we sometimes overreact to things or have counterproductive feelings. We do it out of our genetic drive to protect and satisfy ourselves *right at that moment* without thinking about the future, which may never arrive (remember, prehistoric humans were in constant danger during their time). It's good that we have developed rational minds so we have something else to work with other than our primal instincts. That's what we'll use in counteracting our urges.

The Basic Emotions

As you may have known by now, you can have a hundred emotions. Some people have made lists of emotion words to help people pinpoint what they are feeling. All emotions can be boiled down to 8 basic ones, though. These 8 basic emotions can be further reduced into fewer numbers. I'll explain in a moment.

The eight basic emotions are the following: happiness, sadness, fear, anger, disgust, love, surprise, and interest/anticipation. You may have noticed that they come in pairs: happiness is the opposite of sadness, fear is the opposite of anger (flight versus fight), disgust is the opposite of love, and surprise is the opposite of interest/anticipation.

These emotions may be grouped into two: those that are forms of excitement and those that are forms of distress. Interest and anticipation, both involving paying attention to something, are forms of excitement. Surprise is the opposite of anticipation and interest but it is also a manifestation of excitement. Delight (a pleasurable feeling) is wonderful and exciting, and so are love and happiness. Distressing feelings (similar to excitement but more on the negative side) include anger, sadness, and fear. Disgust is a form of fear (avoidance of something) because it causes you to avoid something repulsive.

Emotion Chart

Excitement							
Excitement				Distress			
Excitement		Delight		Distress		Fear	
Interest Anticipation	Surprise	Love	Happiness	Anger	Sadness	Fear	Disgust

It's important to note that you can pair and group emotions in many ways. In reality, other people have classified emotions differently than what's given here in this book. You need not force emotions to fall under a particular classification if it doesn't make any sense to you. What's important is that you label and organize them in a way that will help you manage them better. Consider other people's structures as mere guidelines that you can modify as you wish, and stick with whatever works for you.

You can feel one or more of these basic emotions at the same time. You may feel complex emotions that are variations of these basic feelings. For example, guilt is composed of fear of what others will think about you, disgust at what you have done, and sadness because you have let people down. Being angry at your child can mean you are afraid that he or she will do the offending thing again in the future, and that you love him or her enough to correct misbehavior for their own good.

The Purpose of Specific Emotions

Happiness. Happiness is a reward. It encourages more of the behavior. Generally, being happy means you gained something that helps you in some way. You need to know that the brain is not naturally wired to keep people happy all the time. Dissatisfaction moves people into action, and satisfaction makes them content to do nothing else since they have already gotten their reward. As you may imagine, if people are already content with everything, they might just as well sit down and die. However that doesn't mean we don't have to strive for happiness, but only that we have to work harder for it, since we are naturally inclined to be dissatisfied for survival's sake. Simply put, happiness is our reward for good things gained.

Sadness. Sadness functions more as a deterrent rather than a motivator. People do their best to avoid being unhappy, because it's an uncomfortable feeling. Although it's distressful to be sad, it helps people reassess their priorities, improve themselves or the situation, and affirm that they have lost something important. The central theme to sadness is loss, which we are inclined to avoid.

Fear. Fear focuses you to the dangers that threaten your safety. The feeling heightens your awareness and produces body changes in you so that you can escape the threat. What's tricky about this emotion is that it becomes active even if the danger is illusory. Fear helps us by making us avoid danger.

Anger. Being angry gives you the impulse to fight something or someone that is making life unpleasant for you. Anger occurs when your boundaries are trespassed – the energy from anger allows you to fight back and protect yourself. Sometimes, anger results to save yourself from feeling emotions that you don't want to have such as sadness or fear. These two emotions imply powerlessness, thus anger comes to the rescue to motivate you to do something about your circumstances. Anger is the drive to fight oppressors and unwanted situations.

Disgust. Disgust makes you avoid something that may harm you. You may not be afraid of feces and dirty garbage but you are compelled to avoid them because they contain germs. This also applies to psychological things like being repulsed when you think about doing something that's unacceptable for you, or when you see other people doing it. Unacceptable things provoke your disgust because they break rules (made by you or by society) that are designed to keep people safe. Disgust is the impulse to keep yourself safe from harm that doesn't scare you.

Love. The purpose of love is to keep people together for their survival and happiness. Love is considered as an emotion that encourages mating, but that's not its only purpose. Mothers love their children and friends love one another not because they want to reproduce, but because love keeps families and groups together, which increases their survivability. There are many kinds of love such as eros (romantic, sexual love), philia (friendship), and agape (unconditional love), to name a few. Acceptance may also be considered as love since you are welcoming something instead of rejecting it. You can also 'love' something so you work to have it. Love is an emotion that draws people and things to you – for the survival of individuals and groups and the passing on of genes.

Surprise. Surprise is a reaction when you aren't expecting something. It stimulates your body to pay attention to the moment so you can remember what happens and learn from it. Humor is a form of surprise because it involves deviating from normality. Humor (which we find acceptable) is enjoyable because it stimulates the brain. Surprise helps us survive through learning from the unexpected.

Anticipation/interest. Anticipation and interest makes you pay attention to something so you can work with it or prepare for it. These keep your mind engaged and your body moving. It makes you look forward to something and have a fun time waiting for it. These two related emotions help with planning for the future and attaining desires.

As you can see, emotions are useful so you don't have to erase them completely from your life. A more practical thing to do is to shorten the time that they affect you, and to reduce the stress that comes with them. Also, if a particular emotion is not helping you, you can choose to feel differently. This book will give you several ways to do those things.

*Emotions are meant to help us survive, but sometimes they backfire and make us miserable. Knowing the purpose of emotion allows you to work on the issue objectively.

How to Know What You're Feeling

Knowing what you're feeling is important because it gives you something to work on. That's why emotional intelligence always include being aware of emotions. Do not suppress or deny your feelings. Emotions have physical components, and they need to flow easily through the body. If you hold them in or fight against them, they will get stuck and have negative effects on your physical and mental wellbeing. It's frequently observed that the more you bottle emotions in, the stronger and more destructive they become once they found a way out. You really need to process them if you want to avoid emotional outbursts that you'll later regret.

If you're struggling with a powerful emotion that you don't want to act upon, simply acknowledge its existence in the meantime. Emotions get our attention because they are built by nature to do so. Once we do notice them, their intensity lowers a bit since they have already done the task of bringing the focus to them. Tell yourself, "I am feeling (emotion)." Labeling and then thinking about what's happening to you makes you use your higher brain functions, which helps you become more objective.

There are times when it's hard to know exactly what emotions are going through you, such as when you're experiencing several of them at once, or when you don't want to acknowledge that you're being affected by a situation. One thing you can do is to pay attention to your body and to your thoughts.

The Symptoms of Emotions

People can feel emotions differently. The symptoms given here are only general descriptions. If you think you're having a particular emotion but your body sensations do not match up with it, it's likely that it's just how you normally feel that emotion. You can also try to analyze the thought to see if there are other emotions lurking behind it.

Happiness

Happiness is a pleasant emotion. The tell-tale sign of joy is of course, smiling. You may feel excited or relaxed when you're joyful – the key feature is that you're enjoying it. Your thoughts will tend to focus on the good things and forget the bad parts. When you're happy, you expect things will be wonderful in the future as well.

Sadness

Being sad is not a pleasant thing to feel. Tears often accompany loneliness. Sad people lack energy, and they may have disturbances in their eating and sleeping patterns. If you're feeling down, your thoughts will center on what's lacking or what's wrong with things. Sadness brings people back to the past.

Fear

Fear changes a person's body so that he or she will be ready to run away and protect him or herself from danger. Fast breaths and heartbeats, tensed muscles, and shaking are signs of fear. It's hard to sleep when you're afraid because your body is primed to be on the lookout for threats. Worry is a form of fear, and fearful thoughts are usually about worrying for the future: that things may go wrong, that you will lose something or that you will endanger yourself. Fear results when you consider the possibility that you won't be able to handle the challenge well.

Anger

Anger is similar to fear because it also gives a boost of energy, but the difference is that you are willing to fight the distressing stimulus. The physical symptoms of anger reflect those of fear since they both involve the activation of the nervous system. However, instead of worrying, your thoughts will be about how the offender has violated what you consider as important, such as your rights, your beliefs, etc. You will then be inclined to hurt him or her back.

Disgust

Disgust is an emotion that expresses disapproval. When you feel disgusted, you feel nauseated, sick to your stomach, and uncomfortable. You frown, wrinkle your nose, narrow your eyes, curl your lips downwards, stick your tongue out, shake your head, lean backwards, and say expressions such as "yuck", "gross", etc. You will think that something is horrible, and you will be compelled to escape and do something to ease your discomfort – such as wash your hands, for example.

Love

Love makes you feel desirous or accepting of people and things. There are different kinds of love, and each of them makes people feel differently. For example, sensual love makes you want to mate with another person, while maternal love makes you want to care for a child. The distinguishing feature of love is that the subject makes you feel good so you want to be with it.

Surprise

Surprise is the fastest emotion to take place. Being surprised makes you jumpy and ready to act. Signs of surprise include inhaling rapidly, widening the eyes, and raising the eyebrows. Some people jump or make sudden movements when surprised.

Interest/Anticipation

Being interested in something that's happening or will happen soon makes you become focused on that thing. Interest and anticipation make you restless, energetic, and attentive. Your thoughts will be centered on the subject of your interest and you may tune out other things that are not related to it. Your facial expression might include smiling slightly and raising your eyebrows a bit. Your voice will be a tad higher and you'll utter sounds like "oh" or "hmmm".

Checking Your Emotion

Apart from paying attention to what you feel and what you think, you can also ask yourself about what emotion/s you have. It may seem silly to talk to yourself, but it's reasonable since your mind has a conscious and a subconscious component. The conscious "you" that is doing the thinking and experiencing is different from the subconscious part of you that is generating the emotions. Acknowledging and communicating with that aspect of yourself will help you manage it.

Accessing the subconscious requires you to be as relaxed as you can possibly get (see next chapter). You have to let go of overthinking since it's your conscious mind at work and not the subconscious. When you have achieved a relaxed attentiveness, ask yourself, "What am I feeling right now?" or "What was I feeling when ___?" Wait for the answer. Do not force the answers according to what you expect or what you think you should have.

If you have ideas of what you're feeling, ask yourself, "Am I feeling (emotion)?" You will know that you're correct if you sense relief or when the emotion makes itself felt, such as sadness results into tears or happiness puts a smile on your face. If not, move on to another emotion and ask again.

You might want to talk to somebody else if you're having problems being aware of and understanding what you're feeling. A person other than yourself will be able to observe you and guess your emotional state if in case you're having trouble discerning it for yourself. A psychotherapist is good at this, and he or she can help you sort your emotions.

*When you give a name to what you're feeling, you give yourself a chance to study it. You can get in tune with your emotional state by calming down, paying attention, and asking yourself if you're feeling a certain way.

Calming Down Emotions

"Calm mind brings inner strength and self-confidence, so that's very important for good health."

- Dalai Lama

Naming Your Emotions

Putting a name to what you're feeling helps you know what to do about it. At the very least, knowing what you're dealing with will calm things down. When you define your emotions, you remove uncertainty, which is sometimes overwhelming.

Relabeling Emotions

Our emotions are made up of what we feel and what we think about what we're feeling. When we label something, we attach other thoughts to it such as what it is, what we can expect from it, and what we can do about it. When you relabel an emotion, you change the meanings associated to it, thus you also alter the emotion's effects upon you.

Here are some suggestions of how to rename an emotion into something that's easier to handle. Create your own list so that you will be ready to switch an irritating emotion into a mild one. For example,

Afraid into Excited

Surprised into Curious

Depressed into Reminiscing

Stressed into Challenged

Dissatisfied into Motivated

Relaxation

Emotions are a form of stimulation. Calming down weakens their physical and mental effects. There are many ways to relax:

Breathing deeply

A fast heartbeat, a common effect of strong emotions, makes you feel out of control. On the contrary, a relaxed heartbeat increases your willpower and concentration. The fastest way to relax is to breathe deeply. Taking deep breaths is often advised for emotional people because breathing affects the body's nervous system, which is responsible for emotions. Slow breathing causes the release of hormones that relax your body organs, thus you become calm. Inhale gradually, hold it for two-seconds or for as long as you comfortably can, then exhale slowly. Do this for at least a minute. Your heartbeat will calm down and so will your emotions.

Progressive Relaxation

This is a widely used technique for relaxing the entire body. You will progressively relax each body part for this. You do this by tensing up the muscles on a particular part of the body and then relaxing it after a few seconds. You can also move it a bit and then let it hang loosely. It's recommended to start sequentially from the top of your head and work your way down to the soles of your feet, or progress upwards from the feet to the crown of your head. This helps ensure that every part is included in the exercise. Otherwise, you can choose any order you want for as long as you don't neglect an area of your body. The relaxed condition of your body sends signals to your brain, which responds by making your emotions calm down to match the state of your body.

Meditation

Meditation allows you to control your thoughts. The more you control them, the better you'll manage your emotions since thoughts and feelings are interrelated. There are many meditative techniques out there, from guided imagery to religious rituals. A simple method is to close your eyes and to limit your thoughts. You can focus on a phrase and repeat it mentally or out loud. You can daydream pleasant thoughts such as pleasant sceneries or exciting plans. You may detach from your thoughts by imagining them to be clouds or soap bubbles that are drifting away from your sight. Choose a method and do it for 5 to 30 minutes. Strive to attain a relaxed yet focused state of awareness when you meditate.

Using Imagination

You can edit your thoughts using imagination. Whenever you're feeling an unwanted emotion, pay attention to how your thoughts play in your head. Tone them down by decreasing the size of visual pictures, removing color, and zooming away from a scene. If you're hearing sounds, mute them, distort them, or make them go completely silent. Turn serious mental movies into ridiculous ones that you can easily laugh about. Do this every time you remember an unpleasant memory – take note that your habits took some time to form, so if you would change them, you have to do it consistently as well.

*Physical sensations and thoughts are intertwined with emotions. You will calm your emotions down when you relax your body and mind.

Processing Emotions

"Emotional intelligence is not the opposite of intelligence, it is not the triumph of heart over head - it is the unique intersection of both."

- David Caruso

Processing your emotions helps in controlling them. Emotions that are neglected often end up worsening. To process an emotion, you need to know where it came from, what its message is, and what its effects are. It will be helpful if you use a journal to make notes about your emotions.

Specifying the Emotion

As mentioned before, you need to know the emotion before you can deal with it effectively. Chapters 2 and 3 help you with this. Choose an emotion and figure out when it started. Write it down. It's better to catch it on the onset instead of letting it simmer in the background and increase in strength without your awareness.

Getting to the Root of the Emotion

Find out what's causing you to feel that way. Transferring your focus from sensations into causes and issues will help you switch into problem-solving mode. Specify the events or subjects that triggered the emotion. Know the thoughts that were generated by those triggers. Bring yourself back to the time when you felt the emotion, or if you are still experiencing it, pay attention to what takes place in your head. List the emotions, triggers and thoughts on your notebook.

Challenging the Thoughts That Fuel the Emotion

Emotions are fueled by thoughts. If you want to stop an emotion from taking control of you, you must not allow it to feed on material that confirm and amplify it. You can only do this by specifying your beliefs and perspectives about the situation. Once you have clearly expressed the thoughts that are linked with the emotions, scrutinize them. Answer the following questions:

Are these thoughts accurate and reasonable?

If the thoughts were correct or useful before, how about now?

What are the evidences that support these thoughts?

What are the evidences that contradict these thoughts?

Will other people disagree with these thoughts? Why? Do their opinions matter?

Are the thoughts helpful to me? Are they harmful? How?

Can I think about the situation differently? How?

Analyze your emotional situation until you break it down to its essential components. See whether your emotions are powered by unhelpful beliefs. Be rational instead of emotional. Do not replay upsetting events repeatedly in your mind. Do not focus on the bad feelings but move on to the practical step of finding ways to help yourself. Understand that thinking about something is not the same as doing something about it. Free yourself from the addictive cycle of ruminating and feeling bad by looking at the bigger picture.

Changing Your Point of View

Things can change if you adjust your point of view:

Looking at the situation from the other person's perspective. Pretend that you're the other person. Are you seeing something new? Can you defend what you're doing? Empathy enriches relationships and opens up perspectives.

Becoming a detached observer. Your involvement in an emotional situation makes you biased. If you're a non-involved outsider, how will you respond? What advice can you give to your emotional self? From an objective point of view, people do things because their internal workings prompt them to do those things. You need not be concerned with whatever's happening with them. Even if they're shouting at you or gossiping about you, it's not about you. You need not involve yourself with their business unless you care about them. Then again, think about whether it's worth caring about these people first!

Moving into the future. Will the situation matter after some time passes, or is it important only when it's happening? You need not waste your time in something temporary. This includes immediate gratifications that set you back from a long-term goal.

Take Action

Your emotions are made by nature to be problem-solving devices so you should ideally solve problems with them. I repeat: ruminating about something does not usually solve anything, unless thinking about it *changes how you feel*. Your actions, whether mental or physical, should achieve something beneficial instead of making the emotions worse. Are you locked in an emotional loop? Snap out of it! Stop the train of thought by doing something random, such as reciting a poem or jumping a few times.

Think about what you should do to make things better for you. Are you envious of someone who you think doesn't deserve the things he has? Let that envy launch you into improving yourself so you can also have them. Question your standards about who has the right to have good things, and release your bitterness by realizing it harms you more than it harms him. In the end, we make our lives easier by letting go of our need to command other people and focusing on ourselves instead.

There will always be things that are beyond our capacity to control. We will regularly come across distressing people and situations, but we can choose to be less distressed about them instead of wearing ourselves out by trying to change or avoid them. Apart from that, there are plenty of things that we could do something about. Focus your energies on the things you can control and don't waste your efforts and time on those you cannot. That is one of the secrets of living a happy and fulfilling life.

Choosing What to Feel

If you don't like what you feel at the moment, distract yourself from the emotions and calm yourself. Chapter 4 discussed that in detail. After that, bring up thoughts and memories that encourage your desired feeling. You can repeatedly say, "I am (emotion)" – doing this triggers your imagination, which affects how you feel. It may take a few minutes before it sinks in, so don't give up early! You may also immerse yourself in activities or situations that bring them to you, such as going to loved ones when you want to feel loved, or watching funny movies when you intend to be happy. Simply acting that you're feeling a certain way can make you feel that way, such as holding a smile for a couple of minutes makes your brain believe that you're joyful, thus you feel joy. The important thing for you to realize at this point is that *you can choose to feel any emotion you like for as long as your thoughts and/or physical sensations are aligned with it.*

Goal Setting and Motivation

Motivation is important in being emotionally intelligent. In everything you do, remind yourself of what's important and why it is so. To motivate yourself, you can do the following:

List reasons supporting the action

List the disadvantages of not following through

Imagine how it's like when you're doing it and experiencing the rewards

Imagine experiencing the discomfort of not doing it

Use the combination of your emotions and imagination to help you achieve your goals. The previous chapters have given you plenty of methods to influence yourself into thinking and feeling the way you want.

Know what you truly want and set goals to achieve them. Designate action steps that bring the goal closer to you. If you're aiming for emotional control, plan how you would react whenever you come across triggers that normally set you off. For example, if you hate yourself every time you make a mistake, plan to take note of the error and then do something about it instead of spiraling into a cycle of depression and helplessness. List disadvantages of holding on to negative emotions: wasted time, sapped energy, missed opportunities, etc. The advantages of releasing unwanted feelings: more time to enjoy the moment with loved ones, a clearer mind, conserved energy, etc.

To keep yourself committed, do not focus on the things you still lack but celebrate what you have and what you have done so far. Find support during challenging times by reaching out to others or finding your inner strength. Simplify overwhelming goals by lowering unreachable standards into achievable ones. Break down complicated objectives into easy, doable tasks and accomplish them one at a time. Control emotions that stop you from achieving goals and nurture emotions that help you reach them.

Remember: we need a bit more effort in doing things for the long term, but we have all that we need to set and get goals.

Expressing Your Emotions Safely and Productively

Unexpressed emotions have the tendency of creating harm as illnesses, sleeplessness, eating disorders, irritability, depression, etc. There are many times when acting upon emotions is impractical or destructive. Save yourself from the negative effects of suppression by seeking an alternative way to release your feelings.

Writing. Putting your mood into tangible words can help clear things out. It allows you to transfer your internal ruminations into something external, giving you the distance you need.

Physical activity. Emotions prepare the body for action. Make it go through the motions without doing something regrettable. Sports and exercise are good for the body and heart because they cause you to expend pent-up energy in healthy ways.

Creative pursuits. Let your emotions inspire you into creating things. Emotions provide writers and artists with valuable material for their work. It doesn't have to be artistic though; any task that requires your creativity can be spurred by feelings, since they color how you perceive things and they give you the drive to act.

Verbalization. Talking with someone gives the triple benefits of letting your emotions out, connecting with others and receiving advice from them. The person doesn't have to say anything in return; just having someone to listen may be enough to relieve your burden. It would be helpful to talk to someone who can give expert advice, though. When talking to the person that makes you emotional, do it to solve the problem together. Do *not* do it out of hurt feelings or annoyance – it will be better for both of you if you remain neutral. Deal with the message and not on how it's spoken. Don't let your emotions dictate how the conversation will go, but let objectives be the priority.

*Processing emotions brings out their goal setting and problem solving benefits while removing their disadvantages. Let your emotions lead you to solve problems instead of irritating them.

How to Apply What You've Learned?

There are some things you can do when plagued by an unwanted emotion:

*Pay attention to what you're feeling

*Calm down and wait for the emotion to weaken

*Do not act if the emotion is prompting you to do something you would rather not

*Do not feed the emotions and avoid ruminating or holding on to the feeling

*Do something unexpected by you and the other person to break the chain of emotion and reaction

*Choose to feel differently by diminishing the unwanted emotion and evoking a desired emotion

*Process the emotion by understanding the emotion's message and using it to solve problems and set goals

*Let go of the emotion by acting upon the situation that caused it and/or expressing it through healthy ways

Practice what you've learned regularly until emotional control becomes a natural part of who you are. You will gain many benefits if you do so.

How To Create More Positivity

This book will give you simple but easy-to-miss ideas on positive living. It will provide key principles and practical steps on how to create more positivity in your life. This book contains the proven and the most effective ideas that will absolutely turn your life around if you apply them faithfully and diligently.

They are easy to understand and follow, certainly doable, and you don't need any special resources other than yourself and an open mind and heart. It is very exciting to know that you are about to read this, as this book promises to make a change in your perspectives about life, happiness, contribution, and positivity in general.

Love Yourself

"Love yourself. Forgive yourself. Be true to yourself. How you treat yourself sets the standard for how others will treat you."

– Steve Maraboli

Loving yourself is the first step towards creating more positivity in your life. Accepting yourself for who you really are, along with your strengths and weaknesses, is essential if you want to live a life of positivity. Acknowledging your strengths gives you motivation, while admitting your weaknesses allows you to have the opportunity to improve.

Contrary to popular belief, self-love is not selfishness or arrogance. It is not thinking of yourself as better than others. It is viewing yourself as capable and complete, ready to love others because you know how to love yourself.

People who love others more than they love themselves are succumbing to low self-esteem. How is this so? They put an extraordinary amount of pressure on themselves to be everything for other people and to please them no matter what, that they spread themselves so thin, they have absolutely no time to care for themselves. This attitude is dangerous as it attracts negativity and feelings of rejection.

Loving yourself produces healthy self-esteem, the kind that doesn't rely on the affirmation of others to also love and do something good for them. It is very important because before any outside force can penetrate your sense of self-worth, you are actually the first person who can sabotage your own confidence.

Here are some ways on how to love yourself:

1. Eliminate negative self-talk

One way of loving yourself is to eliminate negative self-talk. So many people have only themselves to blame for all the pessimism that they are experiencing.

Most of the time, it happens subconsciously as a monotonous commentary going on in your mind. Negative self-talk degrades and paralyzes you, keeping you from reaching your full potential or even simply accomplishing anything. It gives you feelings of inadequacy and depression.

To love yourself, this is the first thing to eliminate.

2. Allow yourself to make mistakes

Realize that everybody makes mistakes, and you are perfect because of your imperfections. Most people have entertained a lot of negativity in their lives just because of their fear of failure. You must not be afraid to fail, as failures are really just ways of not doing something again. Henry Ford famously said, "Failure is only the opportunity to begin again more intelligently." Use your failures as stepping stones to move your life forward.

Fear of failure prevents you from ever trying anything new. This is a very good way of wasting all your intelligence, skills, and talents, which then robs you of all positivity in life. The key is to concentrate on the lessons you have learned from a particular mistake and to find out how to do it better.

3. Have enough rest

You are not a machine. You are a human being, so give yourself sufficient rest and sleep. Sleep restores and replenishes your lost vitality and energy. It also repairs all the damages incurred by the body during all your waking activities.

Also, make time to do things that relax you and calm you down. Spend time on things that you love doing and those which gives you inspiration. Eat the right foods that improve your physical health and get enough exercise. Loving yourself means taking care of yourself.

Love yourself. Avoid negative self-talk and fear of failure. Most of all take care of your physical health.

Live in the Moment

"I promise myself that I will enjoy every minute of the day that is given me to live."

– Thích Nhất Hạnh

Another simple idea of creating more positivity in your life is to live in the moment. Most of the negativity in a person's life is caused by his regrets of the past (hoping to bring back things as they once were or putting the blame of the present to what once was) and the worries and fears of the future (which are impossible to exactly predict).

It does not make sense to regret or hate the past because it is already over and nobody can do anything about it. If you have to think about a sad or an awful past, you should only do so in the perspective of learning the lessons that can be taken from it.

It does not seem right to be anxious about the future as well since no one can truly know what is going to happen. Indeed, it is perfectly okay to prepare for the future, but what is not good is when you get terrified by it. It will be difficult to have progress when you are weighed down by your fear of the future.

Living in the present is essential for a life of positivity. When you live in the moment you are mindful and focused. You are aware, relaxed, and appreciative of what is happening around you. It would be very hard for any negative thing to enter your thoughts as you are focusing on the present moment.

Here are some tips on how to live in the moment:

1. Do breathing pauses

Breathing pauses involve stopping and sitting down for a few minutes only to pay attention to your breathing. Start with two minutes and gradually increase. Most people do have a hard time staying still even for just a minute. Set a timer and breathe in and out while being still. Focus on how the air goes in and out of your body. When you concentrate on your breathing, your mind goes back to the present. Do this several times each day to lessen your stresses and take in some positivity.

2. Notice the small things

Be mindful of anything you do. When you are washing the dishes, just focus on the simple act of washing the dishes. When you are eating, look at the food and savor every bite of it. When you are drinking water, feel its coolness going through your mouth down to your throat.

3. Talk to yourself

This is kind of odd, but it's very effective in bringing yourself back to the present. For instance, again while eating, you can slowly describe the taste and flavor of what is in your mouth. While washing the dishes, tell yourself slowly, "I am washing the dishes." It's a little strange at first especially when there are other people around, but once you get the hang of it, it will feel normal.

Live in the moment. Forget the past and don't worry about the future. Remind yourself by taking daily breathing pauses and always being thankful.

Choose to be Happy

"Happiness is a choice. You are the only person who can make you happy. You're as happy as you choose to be."

– Rick Warren

Happiness does not come by chance; neither does positivity. Actually, everything that takes place in life is dictated by the choices you make every day. Even the seemingly insignificant choices have an effect on what you are and what you will become. It is one thing that is so special about human beings: you always have a choice. And you can choose to exercise that choice in every single moment of your life.

If you want to focus on every trouble, every comment, every wrongdoing that other people did to you, then you can drag your way into life with hate and bitterness in your heart until the day you die. You can choose that.

If you want to focus on being happy, emptying your heart of any negativity by releasing total forgiveness, and living your life according to your passions and purpose, you can choose to do that as well.

Nobody else can make you happy. If that is the case, then you are setting yourself up for a lot of hurts in your life. You have to learn to fill up your own cup, because quite frankly, you are the only person in this world who can do that effectively and sustainably. Happiness has always been internal, not external.

You can choose to be happy by:

1. Waking up with a positive mindset

It is easier to create positivity throughout the day when you begin it with a positive mindset. Realize that there are a lot of reasons to smile and be happy about every single day.

Even little stuff such as a hot cup of coffee, nice weather, and the opportunity to earn a living are things to be grateful for. The mere fact that you still woke up, able to breathe and live, is good news! Build momentum to your day by thinking positive the moment you wake up.

2. Learning to pause when angry

The worst decisions a person makes are always during a time when they are furious. Whether it is something you can say or do, it is always a bad idea to act or react when you are in the heat of the moment. Anger takes away all of the mind's rationality.

Whenever you are angry, try pausing for a second before you say or do anything. Notice that you are out of control by paying attention to subtle body languages like fast breathing and teeth clenching. By doing so, you will be able to avoid any regrettable actions that would lead to more stress and unhappiness.

3. Avoiding comparisons between you and others

Another good way of sabotaging your happiness and self-esteem is to compare yourself with others. Never, ever do that. Keep in mind that you are unique, and there is no other person exactly like you.

There are two consequences the moment you compare yourself with others. One, when you are comparing yourself with someone whom you think is better than you, you begin to harbor thoughts of self-pity, inadequacy, and powerlessness. Two, when you are comparing yourself with someone whom you think is worse, you become arrogant, self-righteous, and deceived. Both paths do not bring any happiness or positivity in life. Avoid them at all costs.

Happiness is a choice. Begin the day with a positive mindset and practice self-control. Realize that you are special so don't judge yourself against other people.

Forgive Quickly

"Life is short, break the rules, forgive quickly, kiss slowly, love truly, laugh uncontrollably, and never regret anything that made you smile."
– Mark Twain

Forgive anyone for everything...and do it as fast as you can. This will create a lot of positivity in your life—perhaps more than you could ever imagine. In truth, forgiveness is for your benefit and not for anyone else's. Holding back forgiveness is essentially similar to drinking poison and expecting the object of your resentment to die.

According to medical studies, forgiveness and its opposite, unforgiveness, is closely linked to not just mental and emotional wellbeing, but also to physical health. Medical practitioners confirm that the negativity caused in withholding forgiveness has a profound effect on the way the human body functions, disrupting its natural rhythms and systems which results in devastating sicknesses and health conditions.

Forgiveness does not only heal you physically, but spiritually as well. Your emotions are kept in check when you constantly practice forgiveness. Holding a grudge makes you think badly of other people, and it eliminates joy, happiness, and positivity in life. Many people have actually wasted years of their lives using their emotions to feed feelings of resentment instead of spending them in living a life of passion.

Here are three main ideas about forgiveness:

1. Forgive everyone and anyone, including yourself

Don't discriminate when it comes to forgiveness. As already mentioned, this is not for their profit. Apply it liberally to one and all without any bias or prejudice. And that includes even yourself.

So many people have fallen into the trap of refusing to forgive themselves. No matter how terrible the things you did, you need to realize that you can be forgiven. Understand that no one is perfect; it's normal that human beings make human mistakes. Sometimes it is actually easier to forgive others, but self-forgiveness is more crucial for a life of positivity.

2. Do it immediately without hesitation

The key to total forgiveness is to give it away as soon as possible. When you let it linger, it plays games with your heart and mind, filling all your thoughts, feelings, and perspectives with negativity. It is like giving refuge to an internal saboteur. It holds you back from accomplishing anything worthwhile with your life as you are consumed with hate and resentment.

The moment a person offends you, forgive him instantly even if they are not asking or would not ask for forgiveness. Again, always remember that forgiveness is for your benefit and not for the benefit of your oppressor. That person may have already forgotten the whole ordeal and moved on, while you are still wallowing in the filthy pool of bitterness.

3. Learn to completely let go

Letting go doesn't mean that you forget the offense and allow the offender to do it again. Letting go is learning a lesson and remembering how you got it without getting hurt anymore. It is actually quite hard to practice genuine anger release, but it is achievable and is one of the keys for a life full of positivity.

Forgiveness is generous and immediate. Give it first to yourself and then to others. Let go completely.

Embrace Change

"Embrace change. True success can be defined by your ability to adapt to changing circumstances."

– Ritu Ghatourey

The only thing that is permanent is change. It is a cliché, but no one can refute its truth. To create more positivity around you, you need to understand that changes happen and they do anytime. Nothing is definitely forevermore.

When you learn to embrace change, you are actually reversing the common victim mentality mindset that changes bring nothing but nuisance and discomfort. Welcoming change will allow you to focus and identify the lessons that can be learned from a specific situation as well as what to do when it happens again.

Your ability to adapt to any kind of situation actually makes you stronger in the long run. When changes are happening all around, you can be the only person that could think rationally.

How do you embrace change? Here are three ways:

1. Acknowledge the possibility of change

Change is sure, whichever way you believe it. It happens quickly and suddenly at any given time without signs or warnings. Be attentive and ready when it comes.

Instead of trying to control change, let it happen when it reveals itself. Especially when it is something that is out of your control. There is no use in denying or resisting it when you can't do anything about it.

2. Don't expect too much

Most of people's disappointments, miseries, and pessimism are the results of too much expectation. When you are always assuming, you are actually trying to resist things to happen as they are, you are opposing reality. Accept that people and circumstances will not always go your way.

People change. They are dynamic beings driven by a lot of factors both internally and externally. You can't manipulate them. If you can't accept that then you should be ready for a lot of pain and negativity in your life.

Circumstances change. There are just some things that are out of your control. You don't have to demand explanation for everything. The rain will not stop for you, nor can you keep a car from breaking down. You must acknowledge the likelihood of disappointments or you will forever be frustrated.

3. Learn to adapt and be flexible

Never put all your eggs in one basket, so to speak. One way to adapt to change is by being flexible to anything that may come your way. Having a lifestyle that is change-friendly will sustain positivity in your soul that is hard to break. It's okay to focus, simplify, and streamline your life. To be so disciplined that nothing can stop you from doing your routine. But being too rigid without any room for adjustments is a formula for unhappiness and despair.

Even when you are focused, still stay open for anything. It's a mark of true maturity. Besides, no one knows what the future could bring. Remember also that not all changes are for the worse. Some may actually be beneficial for you, which you may find out in due time.

Learn to acknowledge and accept change. Lessen your expectations and be flexible.

Find Inspiration Daily

"The good life is one inspired by love and guided by knowledge."
– Bertrand Russell

Inspiration is found in everything, even in the things where you least expect it to come from. The key is to be sensitive to what life is trying to say through daily experiences, realizations, and interactions with people.

Inspiration is actually one of the main factors in driving positivity to a person's life. When your days are full of inspiring thoughts, you will feel like you can do anything you ever wanted. That's how powerful inspiration is. You can continue to go on when everyone else is already tired and weary.

In today's modern society that is fixated with talents and results, people most often neglect inspiration. The dictionary defines inspiration as "the process of being mentally stimulated to do something." This is very important especially when you want to accomplish a goal. Without proper amount of inspiration, all goals are unreachable.

Here are some suggestions on how to seek inspiration every day:

1. Draw inspiration from loved ones

You don't have to look very far to find inspiration. One of the greatest and most common sources of inspiration is your family and loved ones. Perhaps you are not aware of it, but you may already be experiencing it right now.

There are several ways to do this. One is to simply watch them. Looking at your kids can be very inspiring. How many fathers have endured finishing a specific project at work just because they had their children in mind?

Another way is to spend time with them and try to see everything through their eyes. Doing bonding activities with people you love can help inspire you out of the blue.

A third one is talking with them and engaging in meaningful conversation. Ask your spouse what she loves the most about life and observe carefully how she responds with passion and enthusiasm.

These are only some ideas, you may have many more.

2. Fill your life with inspirational media

This is an input/output case in which what you fill your moments with are what you most often experience. If you expose yourself to angry media—books, songs, movies, news, etc.—then you are setting yourself up to be infuriated. If you frequently watch horror films, it is not surprising that you always have nightmares.

What if you fill your life with positive media? What do you think will happen? Listen to inspiring music. Read inspirational books. Watch movies that motivate you and give you hope.

3. Find time for meditation

There are many ways to do this, and it is all up to you which one you prefer. Some people use this time of meditation to just stay still, be quiet, and empty the mind. Others use it for prayer and thanksgiving. There are people who use it for writing, reflecting, and planning. Whatever it is you prefer, this is the time to be alone, contemplate, and release yourself from all outside pressures.

Disconnect from the internet for a while and turn off your smartphone. Find a nice, quiet spot where you can be comfortable, away from the noise of the world. Ponder on your life and think about the little things you have done that made a positive impact on the people around you.

Be proactive in seeking inspiration. Fill your life with it. Have quiet time to reflect and contemplate.

Be Active

"An early morning walk is a blessing for the whole day."
– Henry David Thoreau

Positive people are physically active. Regular exercise not only keeps the body fit but also causes the soul to be happy. It takes you away from a problem physically for a while, and also detaches you from it emotionally, refreshing you as you get ready to face it once again.

Whenever you are anxious about something, you have to give your mind and body an opportunity to step back and turn away from the negativity in order to create an appropriate solution. Physical activity sets off feel good endorphins that will stimulate your brain and give you a more positive outlook.

Exercise also brings you back to the present. As you become aware of the bodily strain of the work out, you become fully in the moment, draining worries and anxieties out. Suddenly, you may find yourself having a realization of what it is you have to do.

Here are some tips on how to stay active:

1. Schedule a regular time of exercise

Whether in the morning, afternoon, or evening, a regular schedule of exercise is crucial to create more positivity in your life. It doesn't have to be strenuous or complicated. A simple daily thirty-minute workout right in your home or a quick run around the neighborhood is enough as long as it is consistent.

2. Play a sport and engage with others

Make time to engage yourself in a sport you love together with other enthusiasts. It can be a team game like basketball, soccer, and football, or individual games such as tennis, boxing, and other forms of martial arts. Having to do it with others adds accountability to the activity, which can help you be more consistent. It is also a great opportunity to meet new friends.

3. Incorporate fitness in your daily routine

You can do this by creating simple habits that add more physical activity in your daily schedule. One example is standing while working. You can have a thirty-minute span where you work with your laptop on a higher desk or table while standing. Another is parking your car all the way to the other end of the parking lot. By doing so, you have the chance to walk further to get to your destination. Another is to take the stairs instead of the elevator. There are many more ideas you can come up with.

Physical activity keeps you healthy and happy. Prioritize it and have fun with others.

Emit Positive Vibes

"The most important thing is to try and inspire people so that they can be great in whatever they want to do."

– Kobe Bryant

Now that you know some of the most important ideas on how to create more positivity around you, you can become a reliable source of positive vibes for other people. You know you are on the right path when you are able to give off positivity than the other way around. There is a saying that you cannot give what you don't have, and this one is a classic example of that.

One of the greatest things you can do for other people is to inspire them to reach their full potential, and giving off positive vibes is a great way to bring out the best in them. By doing so, you will also be motivated and inspired as you see people you can touch change their lives for the better. But it starts with you first.

It can be compared to a glass full of water. You are the glass and the water is positivity. When your life is full of it, time comes that it will overflow and surge out from the brim.

Here are the signs that you are starting to regularly give off positive energy:

1. You are always kind

Your patience is evident, and you don't think ill of others. You do something good for another person without expecting anything in return. You speak softly and gently most of the time, and only raise your voice with authority whenever you want to assert yourself.

2. You are always compassionate

You easily empathize with people and understand their feelings. You don't put that much weight on money anymore, and care more about people. You are willing to gently teach others how to improve themselves. You have a higher sense of ethics, goodness, honesty, and decency than most people.

3. You are always grateful

Whining and complaining now seems so strange to you. You are able to see the good even in the direst of circumstances. You see favors as a privilege and not as an entitlement. You are not afraid to speak compliments. Positive people discern when others are also giving off positive vibes, and they always recognize it and are thankful for it.

Be a source of inspiration. Others need it more than you think.

Make Positive Contributions

"It's not the depth of your intellect that will comfort you or transform your world. Only the richness of your heart and your generosity of spirit can do that."

– Rasheed Ogunlaru

One of the greatest ways to create more positivity in your life is to make positive contributions to other people and the society in general. It's ironic, but most of the time people who have given off the most positivity are also the ones who received them thoroughly and have been benefited with a happy and fulfilled life.

There are many ways to give positively to the world. Here are the steps on how to do it effectively:

1. Know your strengths

First thing to do is to identify the things that you are good at and build on them. Focus on your strengths and continuously develop them. If you are good at writing, cultivate it by practicing daily and attending seminars that will give you more knowledge and improve your craft even more. The same is true for other creative skills such as painting, sculpting, composing music, video editing, and cooking. This applies not only in the arts, but also in sports and other vocations as well.

While there are so many things you can do to make a positive impression, you can create the most impact by using your natural talents and abilities. By doing what you love, you are not only more effective, but you are also most fulfilled by it. Nothing beats the feeling of satisfaction that comes from using your talents to affect positive change.

2. Discover your true calling

A calling is something that you are born to be, and it is something that has to be discovered. You can do so by examining all your past experiences and noticing the direction where your life is headed. Usually, your strengths have something to do with your calling.

Your values and principles are guides in finding your calling and you should list them down. How aligned are these values in your life right now? Does your life reflect these values the way that would have satisfied you? If not, then it is time to act on it right now.

3. Be generous in sharing

Once you have discovered your calling and cultivated your strengths, it is now time to use it for positive contribution. It is perfectly okay to make money out of your talents as there is no better way to earn than working as if you are not working at all. But never put earning money at the top of your priority list. Use your talents primarily to influence the world around you positively.

What is good about being generous with your talents is that, historically, people who had such a lifestyle are often the most successful, wealthiest, and most fulfilled persons who ever lived. For them, it is no longer about the money, but creating positivity that benefits everybody.

Contribute positively to the world using your gifts and talents. Find your true calling and be generous.

Hang out with Positive People

"Surround yourself with positive people and you'll be a positive person."
– Kellie Pickler

Finally, the last idea to be shared in this eBook is also probably the easiest thing to apply. If you want to create more positivity around you, then only spend time with positive people. It's that simple. Stay away from people who are negative, cynical, whining, and pessimistic. You become who you surround yourself with.

Hang out with people who support and encourage you, and who love you as much as you love them. Usually, you can determine these people when you are at the lowest points of your life. Everyone is your best friend when everything is going right and dandy. But the people that matters most are the ones that will be with you no matter what the circumstances are.

Being with positive people sustains positivity in your life as well. It is true that you can't be positive every day. Just like a glass of water, sometimes your positivity also drains from giving off too much. These positive people fill it up back again, replenishing what was lost. A relationship between two positive people is great, as they fill each other's positivity glass up whenever it is exhausted.

Some key points in hanging out with positive people are:

1. Stay away from negative people

Of course, in trying to spend more time with positive people, you should stay away from the negative ones as often as possible. We may not be successful every time, but still be aware if someone is rubbing off negative vibes on you and politely excuse yourself.

Life is too precious to throw away with people who are not treating you right. It is absolutely your privilege as a person to choose the people you want to be with. Hence, choose those who are able to make you happy and smile.

2. Learn how to deal with negative people

There are times when you are unable to easily stay away from a negative person, so it's much better to face them upfront. There are many ways on how deal with a negative person and one of them is to not reciprocate the negativity he or she is trying to impart. You can change the topic or find a third person to join the conversation. You can also avoid talking too much, as the more you speak, the more you ignite the negative fire.

3. Don't be a burden, but be a blessing

It's the same as saying, "Don't be a part of the problem, but be a part of the solution." Once you have found the right company to spend your time with, don't be the one to start giving off negativity in the group. Contribute positively and be generous. Bless them not only with your words but also with your actions. Make it a point that you are someone who can live on your own and be happy on your own, and don't depend on them for your wholeness. Apply the other nine ideas in this eBook.

The best relationships are between people who are independent and are interdependent with each other. Each has a role to play in the group that makes the whole a lot better. Dependent people bring everybody down with their negativity. Don't be such a person.

Find yourself in the midst of positive people. Stay away from those that only bring negativity in your life. Grow to be a blessing to others and not a burden.

How to Apply Key Ideas for the Best Results?

Positivity must start within you before you can give it away to others. That is why the first five chapters of this book talked about strengthening the inner self. Loving yourself, living in the moment, choosing to be happy, forgiving quickly, and embracing change are all necessary to give you a foundation of true positivity. If you are able to master these five principles, the next ones are going to be easy to apply.

Chapters six and seven talked about things that you must do to improve your level of positivity. Finding inspiration daily and being active are important to enhance and sustain the key principles that you have already learned. They are practical steps that you must consistently adhere to in creating more positivity around you.

Finally, the last three chapters deal with how you are going to use your new-found positivity in the real world. By emitting positive vibes, making positive contributions, and hanging out with positive people, you will be able to maximize the positivity that is already in your life. Your life will amount to something and you will not just take up space.

If you will notice, the key ideas presented in this book are best applied chronologically, but don't wait for yourself to master one idea before moving on to the next one. Gradually overlap all ideas together as you go on your journey to a more positive and productive life.

How To Feel Absolutely Great About Yourself

You are a great person. You are even greater than you possibly think.

Oftentimes though, you might feel otherwise. This is quite natural, as there are many things, people, experiences, and situations that could bring you down and make you feel less than who you actually are.

While you cannot change these occurrences and the people and things in it, you can definitely change how you feel. Even if something or someone may have initially made you feel bad or doubtful about yourself and your capabilities, you can still shift away from that. You can make conscious choices to make yourself feel great once again.

Making these choices is what you will learn in this book. In here are 25 powerful things you can do to feel great about yourself. These are very effective because you are not just passively being reminded or told that you are a great person; you are the one actively taking steps to see, feel, and experience how much greater you really are than you think.

These 25 powerful actions take effect as soon as you do them, but they are even more powerful and effective when turned into habits. Make these things a way of thinking and a way of life. Soon enough, you will find it easier to feel great about yourself whatever situation you are in. You will not just be convincing yourself that you are a great person; you will KNOW and FEEL that you are indeed GREAT.

1 - You Are Gifted

Recognize All Your Gifts, Talents, and Skills

You are a myriad of skills, talents, and abilities. You would not have made it this far in life if you did not have any of them. A huge part of who you are now is made up of these skills and abilities that you are gifted with. Surely, you can think of something when talking about these gifts that you have.

When you do not feel so great though, it is hard to summon these wonderful things about you to your recollection. This is why you need to learn this very powerful way to feel great about yourself - that of recognizing all the capabilities that you have.

In order to do this effectively, you need to begin with an open heart and mind. You need to stop if you are preoccupied by thinking of how unremarkable or what a disappointment you are. These discouraging thoughts will keep your heart and mind closed, both containing energies that prevent you from feeling great about yourself.

Get a few pieces of paper, or perhaps a notebook. Better yet, you can even begin a journal. It can be your "Stepping Into My Greatness" journal. Here you will do this powerful exercise, and then perhaps write about everything you think, do, or feel as you read the rest of this book and learn from it.

Now, with your pen and journal, take the time to really think about and write down all the gifts, talents, and skills that you have. Be completely honest. Do not think that you are being conceited or assuming. Feel free to write down all you are capable of. You can even write down related stories or experiences about them. For example, if you wrote about having a skill in fabric painting, you can also write down about that time when you joined a contest and your painted design on a shirt won first prize.

You can begin with writing about simpler, everyday skills, such as repotting plants well, or making the best scrambled eggs in the house, just to get the ball rolling. Doing so will also warm you up until you feel more comfortable writing about your bigger, or even professional skills.

If certain skills or talents surface in your mind and you realize you are not really very good at them, you can either write about how far you have gone in terms of learning them, or you can shift to a different skill or talent altogether. The point is that you focus on what you have and what you can do.

Do this exercise for at least half an hour. Just keep writing freely. Enjoy recognizing the capabilities you have and recalling the stories that go along with them. If you have pictures associated with these things, paste them in your journal too. By the end of 30 minutes, you will have been having fun writing about your greatness and recalling all those good memories.

You can keep doing this exercise forever, but the reason why you are only given half an hour for now is to show you that there is so much more giftedness in you than you think. Maybe you have just not been paying too much attention to how great you are, thus you do not feel so great about yourself. However, now, after having written some of what you can remember about your own capabilities, your hand may have probably started hurting from all the writing, but there are still waves of skills and talents that you have which are racing through your mind, waiting for their turn to be written.

This particular method to feeling great about yourself does not end with this one-time listing of your gifts. Each day, keep writing more. Spend around the same amount of time, or at least for 20 minutes. You can write about the skills you have always had since your were young, or you can write about a skill that you have just exhibited on that day - like maybe you realized that your driving skill saved you from getting stuck in a busy street.

One of the good things about doing this exercise, apart from making you feel instantly great about yourself after writing them, is that it keeps you thinking of and focused on those capabilities that you have. You create a mindset that is oriented towards the positive things about you. Even while you are away from your journal, your mind will have a natural tendency to seek out what skills and talents you have that you can apply or enhance in every situation. You will also feel great about yourself more constantly as your self-recognition of your capabilities becomes a habit.

After a few weeks of writing in your journal, it would be nice and fun to read back on what you will have written so far. You will also discover that even though you may have written so many good things about you and the gifts that you have, more are still coming and surfacing in your mind. As you will see, you have more gifts than you think. Even if you refer to one particular skill that you have, it could have manifested in your actions and your daily life in several ways, thus exponentially increasing your actual abilities and further enhancing that particular skill. You are practically a well of great gifts, talents, and skills, all combined to be a great part of who you are. So, if you want to feel great about yourself, look inside you and let your own gifted greatness make you feel it.

2 - You Are Successful

Acknowledge All Your Successes

Within the next couple of minutes, look back and recall the times when you were able to succeed in something.

You were probably able to remember a few, focusing on the bigger successes. You probably thought of the time when you got promoted, when you won first prize in a sports competition, or when you had your first solo art exhibit.

However, you have more successes than that. Not all of them are as big, but they are still all successes, and none of them are too little. Just think of being able to get up early in the morning and check everything in your day's to-do list. Think of being able to call the friend whom you promised to call. Think of being able to prepare a nice dinner for your family. These are just a few examples of your many, many successes.

Everywhere you look, you will find proof of your success. Look at your planner and there you will see things that you have accomplished for the past week. Look through your computer files and there you will see reports you have successfully presented or short stories you have written during your spare time. Look at the mirror and there you will see how well you put yourself together earlier today.

It is all around you - all these signs of your successes, both big and small. All you need to do is just take a conscious look and really see and recognize them for what they are. Surely, you may have passed by other such proofs of your success in your home or office, but they have faded into the background. It is not because these successes no longer count; it is because you have not been acknowledging them.

Maybe you are looking forward to creating more occasions of success, and that is always a good thing. However, it surely helps when you acknowledge your past successes because they are also reminders that you have what it takes to make success happen.

Of course, when you acknowledge past successes, you do not simply glorify them and become content that you no longer have the drive to create more. Instead, you recognize them and also use them as a reminder that you are capable.

When you let your past successes work for you this way, you will reawaken that feeling of satisfaction about them, and you will feel great about being the kind of person who can be successful about these things. It does not matter if they are big or small; what matters is that they are all part of who you are.

So, moving forward, be more conscious about recognizing proofs of your success. This should be easy because wherever you are, you can be succeeding at something. Even being able to relax in a stressful meeting is a success. Then, when you experience more of these occasions of succeeding in something, feel free to write about them too in your journal. Throw in a few small ones to make it more festive. The point is for you to make it a deliberate effort to acknowledge all your successes, both great and small. Recognizing them all is bound to make you feel great about yourself. It only takes a great person to succeed in them, after all.

3 - You Are Alright

Keep In Touch With Your Inner Self Through Meditation

Things around you may go awry, or you may even be swept by the tension that everyone around you is experiencing during a crisis. You may feel trapped, or cornered, and unsure of yourself. In such cases you may feel helpless, or even useless. When you are in a hostile or tense environment, you sometimes cannot help but feel as though you are at a loss and that there must be something wrong with you for not being able to handle things well. This is even worse when there are people around you who are judging you in the same manner.

In reality, though, everyone may feel the same way in such occasions. The people who are making it worse are just probably more scared than the others, and their way of dealing with the situation is by taking it out on others. Regardless of what goes on around you and what people say, you are not trapped, helpless, or useless. You can get it together just by realizing that wherever you are and whatever you are doing, you are perfectly alright.

Admittedly, that is not very easy to do when you are right in the middle of a crisis or any conflicted situation. For you to easily get into that mindset of Knowing that you are alright, you need to do regular meditations. There are many kinds of meditation, but among its main purposes are to allow you to calm down and to let your mind find that deeper wisdom that lies within you. It is that wisdom that will let you know and make you feel that right exactly where you are, is where you should be, and that you are perfectly alright in it. Hence, there is nothing to worry about, fear, or lose.

Then, with this kind of mindset, you will then be better equipped to determine what needs to be done, or if it is wiser to just stay put and let things take their course until they settle down. You will also not be easily perturbed by events or by what people say. It is not that you do not care or that things do not concern you; it is just that you are able to see how getting all worked up and blaming others do not help the situation or anyone at all. By being able to easily place yourself in a mindset of calm observance, you make yourself the best representation of fortitude in wisdom in challenging situations. Thus, while you are at it, and when you look back at it later on, you would know that you did well, and this will surely make you feel great about yourself.

Now, you need to meditate regularly for you to easily put yourself in the right mindset. As you get more used to being in a meditative state, you can smoothly slip into it even while you are in the middle of a non-meditative environment. You do not really need to do the settling down and the eye-closing during those times, because it is all really just a state of mind. This is when, despite the chaos or hostility around you, you are able to get inside your mind and go deep within yourself, thus seeing everything with a heightened sense of awareness and a deeper level of consciousness. When in this state, you no longer see the people as being hostile to you personally, but as people who are just probably afraid. You no longer see the situation as being tumultuous or troublesome, but probably as a necessity in the course of events in order to clear a path that is meant to be found somewhere along the way.

In short, as you become more adept at reaching deep within you and looking at things from a deeper perspective, you begin to see things more wisely and with better understanding. Thus, you realize that you are in the situation not to be oppressed or made to suffer, but because you needed to experience it for the sake of your own growth and development. In essence, you are truly alright, and you are doing a great job by being fully present and aware of what is going on.

91

So, how do you do this meditation that will help you easily get into that state of mind which helps you recognize that you are perfectly alright? It is quite simple, really. Everyday, either first thing in the morning or before you retire at night, spend at least five to ten minutes in silence. Sit in an upright yet relaxed manner, and close your eyes. Breathe deeply and slowly, and place all your attention in yourself - your breathing, how your body feels, how light everything seems, and how you feel deep inside. Do your best to relax, and to find that place within you that tells you that in the Now, you are alright, you are doing well, and you are great. Focus on these thoughts as you continue to breathe deeply; until such time you feel that you are good for the day.

At first, it may take some time for you to get into that state of being able to focus on the thoughts of being alright and such, but if you meditate regularly, you will be able to shift your consciousness and attention almost instantly as you sit down to meditate. Moreover, even when you are not in a meditative state, as when in a tense situation, you can easily call yourself into such a state, which will then allow you to perceive the situation from a better, calmer, and wise perspective. This is because each time you meditate, you are getting in touch with your deeper self, that part of you that is unaffected and untouched by the physical world and the people in it. This is the part of you that reminds you that despite any situation, you are, truly, perfectly alright.

With this kind of mindset, you need not be troubled so much anymore by what is going on around you. Whatever happens, you know you are alright, and you can easily feel great about yourself for being able to stand well in such difficult situations.

4 - You Do Your Best

Recognize Your Efforts, Whether You Succeed or Not

When joining a competition or aiming for a promotion, you would naturally want to win or earn that award or recognition. Sometimes though, you do not win because probably, your opponent was really that good, or you were just not selected for the new position. While it is natural for you to feel sad or disappointed for not having obtained your goal, there is still reason to feel great about yourself. That is, you still did your best in it. You need to give yourself credit for this. You need to recognize the effort that you put it. You may think that it was not good enough or you did not try hard enough. Whether that is true or not, just think of it as a lesson learned and then do even better next time. For the meantime, however, you still deserve recognition for your efforts and for giving it your all while you were at it. Knowing that you did should make you feel great about yourself.

Moreover, given the fact that you have the mindset that you have to do even better next time, it means that you have not lost hope, and that you still believe that you can indeed do better on the next opportunity. Having that kind of courage, motivation, and inspiration already says a lot of good about you. You should feel great about that too.

Take note that the experience itself - having joined the competition, being a candidate for promotion, or other similar challenges - has contributed so much to what you are, even if you did not get what you are aiming for. It still counts as a significant factor that enhances the person that you are or that you are aiming to be. For instance, you were part of an international competition for a sport or martial art. You may not have won your match, but having had the experience to compete internationally has already increased your level and quality of experience and exposure. Though you did not take a trophy back home, you still brought with you an enriching experience and a greater development that has already significantly changed you as a player or fighter. That is surely something to be proud of and feel great about.

Moreover, even before you have actually joined or expressed your intention to achieve that goal, you need to recognize that you had the courage in the first place to put yourself in that competition or candidacy. You had the courage and the confidence to go for it, and then while you are at it, you gave it your all, and you exerted all the effort you could muster. Regardless of whether you succeeded in your endeavor or not, these steps which you took that lead to that possible success are already worth praising. You went beyond wanting and evolved to Doing - that takes a lot of effort - and you need to recognize your courage, confidence, drive, and hard work. Those are big reasons to feel great about yourself.

So, do not beat yourself up for not having won something or not having been chosen for a promotion or anything of the sort. Sure, you need to learn the lessons and take note of what you should improve on next time; but do recognize that you took the courage to actually go for it, and that you did your best. Be proud and feel great about that.

5 - You Can Do It

Act Right Away

One of the things that can really drag you down is a regret for something that you could have done, but did not. Of course, you do get concerned and held back from taking action especially when you think something is too risky, but there are still occasions when you would have rather dealt with how something turned out than not deal with anything at all because you would never know what could have happened.

Sometimes, you may be held back from doing something not because it is seriously risky, but perhaps because you are afraid to fail or disappoint yourself and others. However, you cannot really know until you have actually done it. Then, even if you realize that you cannot do it well yet, at least you would have known and you would not regret not having tried it. Moreover, even if you may feel a bit of regret for trying it in the first place, you would still have gained a lot from the experience, such as knowing how far you still have to go, and how you would fare if you had done it at another time. In other words, go for it! Act on it whenever you can. Whether excellently or not so excellently, you can still do it. You can always, always try. At best, you will succeed in it and know how you fare in such a feat. Then, there is really no "at worst," because it is not going to be so bad at all. You will learn lessons and know how to improve and what to improve on. Go for it, and it will make you feel great no matter what.

There are other occasions though, when it is not fear or worry that is holding you back from acting or doing something. During these times, you may simply be held back by sheer procrastination or a simple refusal to take the trouble. For example, you have a marvelous idea on using your food photography skills for a small but lucrative project that may eventually bring you even more opportunities of a similar kind. It would be fantastic, as you also really enjoy and love food photography. However, for some reason, you have put off taking action on the idea. It is not because of resource shortage such as lack of time, money, contacts, or materials, but one of those moments when you somehow find a reason to postpone it.

Soon enough, the idea may eventually die down and lose its appeal, or someone else begins to have a similar idea and acts on it right away. The wonderful opportunity has then opened itself to another person, who then opens himself or herself up to the other new opportunities that taking action would have entailed. You may feel just an ounce of regret, or perhaps an enormous one, but either way you might not feel so great about yourself and your idea anymore.

The point is that, whichever phase of life you are in right now, you need to act on your ideas, especially those that have to do with things you really like doing. You can do it, no matter what. You may or may not succeed with regard to the results, but actually taking action, actually doing it, is something you surely can. Sometimes, the action is not even a big one right away, and what is required of you initially is a tiny step that will lead to another. Just take that step and let it open up paths for you.

When you act on things right away, and do not let yourself be held back by fear or complacency, you create more opportunities for yourself. Yes, you may create more challenges too, or perhaps tough lessons to learn. However, in the end, you have enriched your life and your experiences and have built yourself up. As you go through various experiences, you will not be able to help it but feel great with what you have done and how far you have brought yourself forward. You will not be sitting back and wondering about what-ifs, nor regretting why you did not take action right away.

So, go for it. You can do it, in one way or another. You can always manage. More importantly, it will make you feel great, especially in the long run.

6 - You Are Needed Here

Keep Your Mind in the Present Moment

Most worries and anxieties spring from thinking about the future too much, and most heartaches and frustrations spring from thinking about the past. While it is great to recall happy memories and lessons from the past, and while it is responsible to think of the future, it is still best to focus on and remain in the present. Why? Because this is where you are needed.

For you to make the future a promising place, you need to do things now and make a difference now. Whatever you say, think, or do now shall affect what happens in the future, so it is better to keep your mind in the present moment and do what you must while in it. In the present moment, this is where you are, and thus this is where you can be your best, and where you can feel great about yourself.

Of course, looking back at your great experiences in the past can make you feel joyful. However, when you fixate too much on the past, you will soon start seeing the past as the only time when you were really happy, and that now, your happiness relies on recalling that happiness from the past. This is not the case, though. You were really happy in the past, and you can be happy now. That happiness in the past just adds more layer of joy to your current happiness.

How does one feel happiness in the present, especially if the happy occasions were all in the past? You do that by creating your own reasons to be happy in the present, or for recognizing what is already there that makes you happy. For instance, if that joyful experience in the past is a particular celebration about having successfully finished a big project, then for one thing, you can be happy now about the fact that you are that person who is capable of such successes. Then, you can either endeavor to have another idea of a project, or perhaps simply have a small and simple celebration with people who matter to you, just for the sake of a happy get-together. Thus, instead of always going back to the past, you simply bring a piece of it with you, and then you move forward from that time and into the present. After all, there are still more reasons to be happy in the present, more opportunities to take, and more celebrations to enjoy. Bring it all to the present because this is where you are now. This is where you can make a difference. This is where you can feel great about yourself again.

Looking back at the past constantly only gives you a reminiscent taste of what you experienced back then, and you may keep trying to recall it because you may find it hard to let it go. In the same manner, you may keep thinking about the future and your dreams for it. You may feel excited about the things you will have and the places you will go to and the person you will become. You like visualizing these things because you might feel that if you do not, you might lose that feeling of excitement.

In both these examples though, you are not actually living in the present moment. Sure, both scenarios - past and future - make you feel great. When you need to return to the present though, there can be a slight pang of having to leave the past behind or having to let the future seem all distant again. Your current scenario or life may suddenly seem bland compared to the past, or simply be cluttered with a lot of chores and tasks compared to the visualized future. The thing is, it does not have to be like that. The reason why you need to keep your mind in the present moment is for you to quit comparing it to the past or future and feeling bad about the stark difference.

Instead, given what you have now, use it and do what you can with it. Create that desired future with what you do now. As you go along, you will become more and more used to it - getting things done and continuously moving toward the future, one conscious step at a time. Right here, in the now, is where you are needed. It is where you take responsibility for what the future will be. In the present, you are neither preoccupied by worries about the future or by the imagined successes in it, nor are you trapped in the past. You create the now and the future, and as you gain more experience and confidence in every Now, it is also the time when you recognize how great you can really be, right Now.

7 - You Do Things Well

Do Everything Well

Doing things well is always an effective way to feel absolutely great about yourself. The key to doing things well is to be competent, and not competitive, about it. When you are being competent, you are utilizing the skills and capabilities that you have in order to perform the task successfully. This is regardless of who observes the way you work or sees your output. You are doing the task well simply because you have the ability to do things well.

On the other hand, when you are being competitive, you are making yourself do the task well, because you are putting more weight on winning, on being better than others, on being praised and recognized by others for your efforts and skills. You are doing the task and making sure you do it well, for the sake of an audience, whether there is an actual audience or a perceived one. In this case, you are still very capable of doing the task well, except that your satisfaction and validation relies on what other people say. You then put the power of feeling great about yourself on the hands of others. When you do it this way, you will never feel truly great about yourself because you will simply be functioning under an imagined microscope through which everyone is looking at you and constantly giving feedback.

This is why this method tells you to simply "do everything well," not, "do everything well to win," or "do everything well to gain praise or validation from others." To really feel good about yourself, you just do the job well, simply because you do things well. There may or may not be an audience; your output may or may not be placed under review or scrutiny. Regardless of the situation, just do what you need to do, and do it well. Any praise, recognition, or reward that comes because of it is just a bonus, but it is not your aim or purpose. Your reward is the ability to do things well, along with the satisfaction that goes with it.

Some people do not care to perform tasks well because they tend to think that it is all for nothing, that no one will notice anyway, or that there is no point because people do not care. These people think that way because they do not see their own value as being the one who can do it or as being the one who can make a difference by doing it, even if in just some small way. They also do not see the value of building their own skills and abilities, and the value itself of doing things well. Rather, they put their value on what they think will give them a sense of importance, validation, or purpose - and these are often things that they can show off or tell other people about, such as money, awards, recognition, praise, or anything that will make them feel that their efforts did not go to waste because they had an audience who will know of what they did.

When you truly do things well, however, it will not matter if no one ever finds out about it, or if you are all alone in the room. If you are the kind of person who does things well out of your own volition or as an expression of your own values, and not because you seek an audience who will praise you, you are the one who will definitely be able to feel truly great about yourself. This is because you know within yourself that you have the ability to do it, and hence you just do things well - no audience or validation necessary. You just do.

8 - You Are Complete

Be Thankful For Everything That is In Your Life

Being thankful for everything means focusing on all that you have at any given moment and being happy and grateful for having them. Most of the time, people say their thanks when something great, big, and fortunate happens along their way, and this is a good thing. However, how about all those times in between when there are no such apparent great, big, and fortunate events or things taking place?

You can be thankful for even the smallest things, and this mindset of being thankful for everything will greatly influence how you feel about your life, and how you feel about yourself. Look around you. There may be no great, big things happening to you right now and there may be no new, shiny things in your possession, but you still have every reason to be thankful. You have your life, your health, your skills and ideas, all inside your body and mind. You have his book, the chair you are sitting on, the sounds you can hear outside. The nice weather, the food that awaits you on your next meal, the clothes you have on your body. There are countless things and experiences and feelings you can be thankful about. It does not just have to be the big things, but also the small ones that you may not even notice because they have been part of what keeps you going and makes your life comfortable.

As you begin to pay more attention to the things around you, to what you have, and to every single detail in your life that you should be thankful for, it then puts your entire self and entire life into a different perspective. You begin to see how great it is to be you, after all. You realize that all these things that you are thankful for, make up who you are. In short, you and your life are made up of things that you can actually be thankful for.

Even if you look at the parts of your life that do not seem favorable or pleasant, there is always something in them that is hidden from your view, but which you should still be thankful for. Oftentimes, these seemingly unfortunate events have a way of either working out fine, or of opening a path that leads to a better way of life or to better opportunities. Anywhere you look, there is always something to be thankful for, and when you recognize all these things and begin to live life with a thankful attitude and mindset, it leaves you no room to feel bad about yourself and your life.

Furthermore, when you are being happy and thankful for what you have, it takes away the occasions of being sad about what you do not have. Being unhappy or angry about not having certain things or a certain way of life is the opposite of being thankful. It is perfectly alright to want more things or to wish for a better way of life, but that is where the inspiration to do something should spring from. When you are thankful about what you have and at the same time you aim for more, you simply become inspired by your natural inclination to keep doing better.

On the other hand, when you are embittered by what you do not have and you feel sadness and anger for not having them, then you are neither being thankful and cognizant of what you already have, nor are you doing anything significant to actually obtain what you do not have. That absence of thankfulness robs you of the will and inspiration to act in order to obtain what you want, thus you stay unhappy and bitter about not having them. A thankful mindset and attitude though, magnifies what you do have, and inspires you to act on what you wish to improve or have more of. When you are thankful, you feel great about yourself and your life, and you can move forward with ease to find more things to be thankful for.

9 - You Are Positive Company

Visualize Yourself As Bringing Peace Wherever You Go

Visualizing yourself a certain way influences how you think, speak, and act. If you visualize yourself as a good host or hostess in a dinner party, you are likely to act out the way you imagined yourself to be. If you visualize yourself as being polite and pleasant around a certain group of people, you are more likely to act accordingly when in the actual setting. Basically, when you see yourself a certain way in your mind clearly, it becomes some kind of mental practice for you. When you are in the actual scenario, you become what you imagined yourself to be.

In the same manner, when you visualize yourself as being the kind of person who brings a peaceful, cheerful atmosphere with you wherever you go, you do bring that kind of energy with you into a place. When you walk into a room with a group of people in it, they will not be antagonized nor be wary of your presence, because will be more of a positive, pleasant company to have around. This applies both for people whom you know and those you do not. Even if you do not say so much, your natural movements and expressions will be that of a pleasant company, because you have visualized yourself as the kind of person who brings peaceful energy with you.

How do you visualize yourself as such? Basically, you let yourself become relaxed and open. You let go of all preconceptions about people, judgment, resentment, and defensiveness. When you are empty of these things that can hold you back from connecting openly with others, you then let yourself fill up with warmth and cheerfulness that are intended for sharing with others. Hence, you become filled with welcoming energies instead of those that defend and shun.

You can do this visualization even as you are going about your daily tasks, and even if you are all alone. It is generally a disposition that naturally becomes a part of you as you consciously make the visualization a regular practice. Thus, when the time comes that you need to interact with people, you are not merely putting on an act or a "social mask" that needs to be shown when you have company. You are simply being what you have visualized yourself to be - someone who exudes an aura of peace and a pleasant attitude that can influence the atmosphere you are in.

With this kind of disposition, it is not just the people around you who feel better and more comfortable having you around; you yourself would feel pleasantly calm and confident being around different people. You would feel great about yourself because you are able to create good company for yourself by being the same to others. Most importantly, you just naturally feel good and peaceful.

10 - You Are Kind

Always Look For The Good in Everyone

When you look for something good in anyone, you will always surely find it. No matter how small or seemingly unimportant or insignificant, you can always find something good in people. Then, when you have found that goodness, focus on it and keep it in mind as that person's "highlight." Whenever you think of or interact with people, remember or recognize them for these highlights. As you do this, you will discover that they have more of these good things in them, until the way you see them becomes more and more oriented towards the positive.

Always choosing to recognize the good in others influences the way you think of, feel about, and interact with them. This results not only to better connections and relations with others, but also a natural tendency in you to exhibit the good that you have. As you consciously choose to think of and focus on the good in others, your own goodness also comes forth, and you create a positive connection between yourself and them. As you become kind to people by acknowledging the good in them, your own kindness radiates from you.

Kindness shown to others that is reflected back to you will always make you feel great about yourself. It is not out of pride or a sense of self-righteousness. It is more about feeling great because you are making the right choice each time of choosing to see the good in others, and thus you help yourself have good relations with them. Of course, when your interaction with others goes well, you free yourself from unnecessary conflict, tension, and offense to others. You create better communication and relationships. At the end of each interaction, you walk away feeling great about it, especially when you know that it is mostly due to how you chose to see others which then influenced how you interacted with them. You did well and that would always make you feel great.

11 - You Are True to Yourself

Pay Attention to How You Feel

When a close friend of yours is preoccupied or sad but tries to hide it by acting cheerful and normal, you oftentimes still see through it. You usually ask how he or she is, what is wrong, or if there is anything he or she wants to talk about. You do this because you are concerned about your friend, and you want to be able to help or at least contribute to making your friend feel better. You ask because you want to know if your friend needs your company especially at that moment, or perhaps if you should give him or her some space. Basically, you pay attention to what your friend feels so that you can address what is needed.

In the same manner, you need to pay attention to your own feelings. You need to keep in touch with yourself through your emotions, and how you truly feel about things. Sometimes you may bottle up an emotion because you perceive it to be wrong, insensitive, or even cruel. However, whatever these feelings are, they are there; they are neither right nor wrong, and they need to be addressed.

If, for example, a colleague who slacks off and makes your work even more difficult gets fired for his work ethics and a few other disciplinary cases. Some people around you express how sorry they feel for him, and they all seem sad about seeing that colleague go. However, in your case, you do not feel any sort of sadness. What you feel is relief and a tinge of joy, not because your colleague got fired, but because now you have a better and easier working environment.

You may feel ashamed for feeling something so selfish, and then try to convince yourself that you are really sad and that you wish your colleague did not need to be fired. However, your mind has to do extra work in order to convince yourself that this is how you feel, so you become confused and you lose focus. At the same time, you start feeling that you are so mean to not feel sadness for others getting fired, until you end up with an unclear stand on the issue. In the end you feel even worse, and you are not sure anymore what you feel bad about.

While it seems mean that you do not feel sad for your colleague, it does not mean that you rejoicing at his misery; you are just probably so intent on your goals and your tasks that you recognize the fact that you do not need any additional worries or burdens through difficult colleagues. Moreover, the joy that you feel is mainly for the improved working environment, and not because someone got fired. Nothing is directed personally at the colleague. Hence, while it may seem wrong to others, you need to see the fact that this is really what you feel. Maybe you cannot talk about it to everyone, but if that is how you feel, then let it be so.

When you are honest with yourself about how you really feel about things, it will be easier for you to analyze why these feelings are such, where they are coming from, and what actions they entail. You do not go through an internal conflict between how you really feel and what you should feel. You just know how you feel, you accept it, and then you deal with or act on it the way you should. In the example above, the action your feelings entail is just that of moving forward with the tasks as usual, but now with more ease.

You do not need to explain to anyone why you are not as sad as everyone else, and why you can easily get back to a normal work pace after what happened. You just stay true to how you feel, think about what must be done, and get on with it. At the end of it all, you will realize how much easier you made things for yourself, because you just saw things with clarity and acted accordingly. So, pay attention to what you really feel and listen to it; you will feel absolutely great about yourself because you will not place yourself in conflicted situations or internal struggles, and you did not let others dictate to you how you should feel in a situation. You became true to yourself.

12 - You Know What You Need

Listen To Your Own Needs

Apart from paying attention to how you feel, you also need to listen to what your real needs are. Usually, your feelings are the ones that will give you a clear idea of what these needs are. You will either feel a strong urge to do something, or you will experience a certain discomfort that will prompt you to change something. These are your body's ways to tell you that you need something, and that you should address it soon.

The strong urge to do something may sometimes be inexplicable or even unreasonable, but you feel it in your gut that you do not just want to do it, but you need to do it. For instance, while at work, you suddenly have a clear idea about going on a particular trip, and the idea is accompanied by a strong gut feel that despite the abruptness of the idea, this is what you need to do. It is not the season yet, but you feel strongly about it. It may not be clear yet what the need for a vacation is, but later on, after having taken it, you realize that it was a signal of your body to you that you need to take a break and step back from everything. It turns out you do enjoy your work, but you realize you had not rested or taken a break in years.

Sometimes, the signal comes in the form of a discomfort. For instance, while hanging out with your usual group of friends, you notice that you are starting to feel some discomfort when hanging out too long with some of them. You experience a drain in your energy and a sudden feeling of insecurity and uncertainty. Then, it all goes away when you are alone or in the company of others. This could be a signal to you that it is time to change your environment and friends, or at least some of them. It could be due to growing differences, or that maybe you realize deep inside that you no longer share the same values. In this case, it is time to follow what you feel and seek a better group or company.

When you listen to your own needs, you become able to address them right away. On the other hand, if you ignore them and just insist on going through the same things again and again, then the discomfort will increase and the urges will turn into a discomfort themselves. You will feel that there is something wrong or not in place but you somehow cannot place it. As you try to live life as you have always done, the discomfort only increases because your real needs are not being met. You need to ask yourself; do you need to be alone for now? Do you need to review that new schedule you are following? Do you need to talk about your relationship? Find out what you need. In fact, you know it already, hence the signals your body gets. You only need to address it. Then, just like any satisfied person, you will surely feel great about yourself. You are content, you are fine.

13 - You Are Driven

Focus on the Things That You Are Aiming for

When you constantly think about the things you want to achieve, your actions will be inclined towards getting closer to them. Your senses become more sensitive to relevant information and open to more opportunities that may lead you to them. Your interests and activities will gravitate towards the things you wish to achieve. In the process, you will meet people, encounter situations, and learn lessons that will drive you even more towards your goals.

More specifically though, you need to think of the things you want to achieve in the context of already achieving them. If you think of the things you want to achieve and how impossible it seems or how hard it is to get there, then you will never get there. Instead, awaken that drive inside you that will bring you to your goals by focusing on what you want to achieve and on actually getting there. The exact manner or process of getting there may already or may not yet be clear to you, but what matters is that you have set your mind towards what you want to achieve and seeing yourself achieve it.

As you do this focusing and visualization, you will constantly see yourself as being able to get to where you want to be, and that is a major contributor to your feeling great about yourself. When you feel great about yourself, the more motivated you are to move towards your goals. You also gain more confidence and courage to grab opportunities when they arise. Thus, focusing on your goals and feeling great about yourself work together for you to be able to do both.

14 - You Are Supported

Expect the Universe to Be Generous to Your Needs

When you believe in something, you imbibe that belief with positive energies. In the process, you empower it with such, and so the sooner and likelier it happens or comes to you. When you believe that the Universe supports you, the more you will experience how things work out for you and how paths become open to you so that you can get to where you want to be. In the same manner, when you believe that the Universe is generous to you and provides you with what you need, you will experience how your every need is met in one way or another.

It is basically a process of releasing positive thoughts to the Universe, and so these thoughts are manifested back to you in various forms. Whatever form they are, they are always in one that suits you best at any given time. So, when you need something and you believe that the Universe will give it to you, you will get it. It may or may not be in the same form that you expected, but you will get it, if not a better version of it.

As you continue to believe that the Universe responds to your needs, you will feel even more that you are supported. You may be one of millions of people asking for their needs to be met, but you are not lost among those millions. In your own way, you are special, you are supported, and your needs are being heard and met. Remember this, and recognize how this has come true for you in various occasions. Know that this support will continue as long as you believe. When you do, you will naturally feel like someone who really, truly matters - and that can easily make you feel absolutely great about yourself. You matter,

you are not forgotten, and you are being heard and
supported.

15 - You Care For Yourself Well

Take Care of Yourself

Taking care of yourself well ensures that you feel great about who you are. It means that you value yourself and that you deserve proper care. This does not only refer to physical care, but mental, emotional, and spiritual as well. By making sure that all these aspects of you are well taken care of, you are contributing to an overall feeling of well-being, self-appreciation, and a great confidence.

However you treat yourself also sends out a signal to others. It tells them how they should also treat you. When people recognize, whether consciously or unconsciously, that you know how to take care of yourself well, they will approach you with the appropriate manners that they perceive you deserve. Thus, how well you take care of yourself will elicit the same kind of response from others, and that shall affect you accordingly. This means that how you treat yourself will determine how you feel about yourself, hence caring well for yourself will result to you feel great about you.

Of course, just like most people, you do want to be treated by others well. However, there are times when people still treat you in ways you do not prefer them to. Setting aside those who are purely unable to socially interact, these people may be unconsciously treating you a certain way because of how you care for and carry yourself.

How you carry yourself is also part of how you treat yourself. If, for example, you treat yourself as someone who is confident and capable of doing something really well, it will show in how you carry yourself through your posture, the way you talk and act, and how convinced you are that you can do it. When others can sense that you do know what you are talking about, they begin to regard you with more faith and respect.

If they sense you faltering however, they will regard you with less respect and confidence, and thus treat you in a way that will make you feel even more unsure and insecure. While this can be a harsh reality, some people may be doing this to you unconsciously. It is not a personal attack on you that they are not relying on you fully; it is just that they can sense that you may not exactly be who they are looking for. So, if this happens, you go back to how you care for yourself. Why do you not sound confident when talking about a matter that you are supposedly knowledgeable about? Look back at what you may have done wrong or perhaps, what you are not doing about yourself. Maybe, you may discover that you cannot exude the confidence you wish you had, because you yourself are not treating your own self with the same faith and confidence that you would like others to have on you.

You can then go back further and see why you are not as confident with yourself as you would like to be. Perhaps it is due to an admitted lack of experience or training. In this case, you should then take better care of yourself by enrolling yourself in a class or training session. Maybe you are not as confident because you realize that you simply do not look and sound convincing. To address that, you take better care of yourself by asking for help on how to improve your communication skills. You may also revisit your personal style, and find one that makes you feel superbly confident and comfortable. It all boils down to how you care for, package, and present yourself. When it clearly shows that you are thorough and sure about who and what you are, it will elicit from others the faith, support, and respect that you have given yourself. Therefore, take really good care of yourself, in order to feel great about yourself.

16 - You Are Capable

Have Faith in Yourself

Having faith in yourself and feeling absolutely great about yourself go hand in hand. You may not have mastered the skill you want to master, or you may not have reached your financial goals yet, but you can still do both - you can still have faith in yourself that you will be able to master the skill and reach your financial goals. At the same time, you can still feel great about yourself. You can do so because you know that you have the capability and the patience to do what it takes to master skill. You also know that despite the difficulty, you are still taking the necessary steps to achieve your financial goals.

The concept of having faith in yourself does not only happen after you have proven to yourself that you can do something. The fact that you have faith means that even without the proof, you know deep within you that you have what it takes to accomplish something. You also do not only feel great about yourself after you have succeeded in doing something. You can do so even before the event, because you know that you are brave enough to move forward and that you have the drive and ambition to improve your state or situation.

So, have faith in yourself. Do this by recognizing all the gifts and abilities you have, and know that you have the capability, the will, and the strength to use them in order to achieve something. Even when you fail or make mistake, keep this faith in yourself. Mistakes and failures are not the end of everything. You can always get up from them and move forward again. Moreover, when you have true faith in yourself, you know that even when faced with difficulties and challenges brought about by mistakes, you have the discernment and the strength to recognize your mistakes and thus learn from your unfavorable experience. You have faith in yourself that you will not give up easily or succumb to fears and anxieties. When you have faith in yourself, it immediately follows that you do because you know how great the person is that is inside you - and you feel great about that person. You have faith in and you feel great about you.

17 - You Deserve Good Things

Be Accepting of Help, Compliments, and Gifts

Be open to help, compliments, and gifts in various forms. Know that you deserve good things. When you see yourself this way, it becomes easier for you to feel great about yourself. After all, you are a person who is being given good things because you deserve it.

Accept compliments graciously. You are not being arrogant by saying a simple thanks and perhaps a quick mention of someone who helped you succeed or contributed to whatever you are being complimented for. However, do not over-thank nor try to dissuade someone from seeing you as worthy of compliments even when you feel you deserve it. False modesty is not the way to go, nor will it make you feel great about yourself. It will make you feel uptight and the contrast between your words and feelings will cause an unnecessary discomfort.

When you accept compliments graciously, you are putting yourself in an even better light, which will further make you feel great about yourself. Looking back at the moment, you will feel pleased by the compliment, and you are more deeply pleased at how you handled it. These are additional points for your true greatness.

Being accepting of help may not always mean actually accepting the help offered. You may take it if you really need it, but if you feel that it will be of trouble to others and you can do it better alone, you may very politely and nicely decline. Being accepting is not just a matter of actually taking what is offered, but being very clearly appreciative of it. Hence, when you decline, you can either clearly express your appreciation, again, without over-thanking. At the least, you may ask for just a little assistance or allow the person to partially help, just so you were able to give him or her the pleasure of being of help. In any case, these offers are often signals that you are someone who deserves such offers of kindness. Refrain from thinking that you are being offered help because others perceive you to be weak or incapable; it is not a mentality that will help you feel great about yourself.

Accept gifts graciously as well. Give back expressions of thanks such as cards or gifts too, depending on the circumstances. Remember that even if a gift is not something you would prefer, recognize the fact that you were still found to be of importance or to be someone deserving of a gift. Whether the giver's intentions were sincere or functional, focus on the idea that you were still given a gift, recognized, and that you deserve it in your own way.

18 - You Are Focused

Have Clear Plans for Your Dreams and Goals

When you have a fair amount of control of things, it gives you a sense of responsibility and a certain level of satisfaction. Being in such a state automatically gives you as well a certain feeling of greatness, which can be increased or enhanced when you maintain having this fair amount of control.

You can only have a fair amount of control of things because in reality, anything outside of you is mostly beyond your control. Thus, you focus on what you can control. When it comes to the fulfillment of your dreams and goals, you do this with the plans that you have, and the actions that you take out of them.

When you have clear plans and a moderately sure way of getting things done, you develop a stronger sense of control and thus the greater you feel about yourself. You will be able to see that as you fulfill one task to another and move forward with your goal fulfillment, you are focused, motivated, and fully capable.

In the event that a plan goes awry and your progress comes to a halt, you may momentarily lose control of things. However, if you let that aspect of you that is focused and clear with what you want to take the lead, you can still move on and get back on track. When you do this, you bring your feeling of greatness to an even higher level than before.

Thus, after encountering such difficulties and challenges, you are even more motivated and encouraged. You become more capable to either create new plans that are under your control, or pick up where you left off, but braver and stronger this time around.

19 - You Are In Good Company

Surround Yourself with People Who Make You Feel Great

What you surround yourself with has a great influence on how you feel about yourself. If you are constantly with people who are often problematic, depressed, or insecure, they might pull you down with their energies and thus you are often drained after spending time with them. What is worse is that because they feel negative, they may even say unpleasant things about you or disparage you one way or another. Clearly, this kind of environment will not make you feel good about yourself.

On the other hand, if you are always spending time with people who are happy, successful, driven, and supportive, you will imbibe the same values and attitude. Moreover, because they are supportive of you, they will often bring to your attention the things that are good about you, thus contributing to how you feel about yourself.

Take note though, that when you surround yourself with people who make you feel great, make sure that they do it because they are great people themselves who support great people like you. Do not simply go for company that makes you feel great because they regard you as the highest among them - very similar to the attitude of fans towards an admired person. Go for company that can offer you more than mere admiration, but also a sincere support and acknowledgement of the great person that you really are.

20 - You Are Provided For

Work with What You Have

Many disappointments and frustrations in life spring from the dissatisfaction of not having enough things or not having one's needs met. This perceived lack becomes an obstacle to getting things done or moving forward with work and life. The truth is, the Universe provides you with what you need. If there are specific things that are not available to you, it means there are others that are. The idea is for you to be able to work with or utilize what you have. You shall see that what you need is what is already provided for.

Learning to work with what you have also increases the sense of control that you have over things. You know how to maximize the resources available to you and you become enabled more quickly to get things done because you can adjust based on what is given to you.

Working with what you have also shows you that you are not lacking in anything; hence you become busy with and focused on the work, and not on the complaint about not having this and that material or item. Then, it teaches you to be flexible with your resources and hence, you waste no time and energy waiting for other things that you claim you need to be present before taking action on a task.

For example, you wish to start small life coaching sessions, and all you have for them are a small room, some office supplies, and just three people who are interested to be among your first clients. You would have wanted a bigger office and more impressive furniture and supplies, along with more clients, but right now this space is what is available to you. So, you work with it. You occupy the small office and try to make it as cozy as possible, then you take care of those three clients as much as you would if you had a bigger office or perhaps a bigger name as a life coach. This is all you have now, so you work with it.

When you learn to work with what you have, you will not have idle time that went to waiting for the desired setting, items, and opportunities to show up. You would just do what you can right away, whatever resources are available. You no longer seek out what is not there. You work with what is there at any given moment. Doing this gives you the knowledge that your needs are provided for, and that there is enough for you to work with. Knowing this and how to manage what is available does make you feel good, because you know that you will not be trapped or slowed down by any perceived lack or the inability to work with only what you have.

21 - You Are Wise

Always Choose to Do the Best Thing in Each Moment

Various situations call for different actions and solutions. Sometimes, there are ideal ones that you would wish to take, but the circumstances do not allow it. Hence, you need to decide on and to do the best thing that you can do for the situation. Sometimes these actions require hard work or extra effort than usual, so that resorting to other options is considered. The other options may work, but not all the time. If they do work however, it would mean less effort.

In such cases, it is easy to be drawn towards the easier solutions or actions, hoping that it would work out somehow. However, if you want to feel absolutely great about yourself, choose the best thing that you can do for each moment. You are a wise person and you have learned many lessons from the past. You know that choosing the best course of action shall leave no room for regrets and ensures the best results. It may require more effort or work, but finishing it all later on and knowing that you made a wise choice shall definitely make you feel as great as you can be.

22 - You Are Wonderful

Remember All Your Virtues and Best Characteristics

Remembering all your virtues and best characteristics can be an easy way to make yourself feel great - it reminds you that you are a wonderful person after all. However, it does become tough when you have just experienced a rejection, a negative comment, or reproach. This can be difficult, especially when it concerns the opinions of a person who matters a lot to you. While it may hurt, though, you need to remember that these occasions bring lessons with them. Perhaps there is something you need to adjust about yourself; it is also possible that the other person just does not appreciate you as much as you would like them to, but you are wonderful just as you are.

Regardless of how others may be towards you, you need to be the first person to appreciate all your virtues and best characteristics. Write them down if you must, and think of specific circumstances when you displayed them. See yourself as being each of those virtues and characteristics, and know that no matter what happens outside of you, you are fine, and you are that wonderful person made of these impressive qualities.

23 - You Are Smart

Read, Learn, and Never Stop

This is one way of feeling great about yourself that requires continuous work and effort. It is not as hard as it sounds though, so even if you do it until your last days, it would not be as tedious as you would imagine. You need to read, learn from reading, and never stop.

When you read and learn a lot, you do not only become more knowledgeable about things, but you also develop a certain character that exudes with smartness and confidence. You speak and write better, and you understand spoken and written language more easily. When you join in a conversation or a discussion, you have a wide range of references and collected information that you can use to your advantage.

Being in such a position of being well-read and knowledgeable distinguishes you from those who may have learned a lot of things but hardly read. You can learn things outside of reading, but reading is among the most comprehensive and effective ways to learn more about various things. You can go back to a book and make notes, and even expound the information through your own ideas and writing.

You may not always say a lot or participate in various conversations, but you will feel the difference in your perception and absorption of information and development of insights as you listen to others talk or observe their body language. You can get more out of simple discussions when you are so used to reading and absorbing information, than when you are always just listening and trying to remember later on.

The effects of being well-read and learned can always give a boost to your great feeling about yourself, so start reading more starting today.

24 - You Are Loved

Never Take Things Personally

Do not take offense easily when you are not selected for something, when you are ignored, snapped at, or when something you said was forgotten. All these situations may be irritating, and this irritation may easily pass and be forgotten. In some cases though, you may find yourself taking a comment too personally, or feeling as though a forgotten restaurant order of yours is a personal attack on you.

Sometimes, people say things that end up hurting or offending you. Sometimes they say it to hurt you, because that time, they were really frustrated or angry. Usually though, they either did not mean it, or only meant it for you to do something about it. In some cases though, something wrong is done and you happened to be at the receiving end of it. Do not immediately think or assume that you are being attacked or that everything is not working out for you because you are not likable, you were mean, or you are not popular. Even if the weather does not agree with your expectations, do not think that you are being punished by the heavens for whatever reason.

These unfortunate incidents do not always have to do with you nor are they about you. Sometimes you just happened to be there hence you were the one shouted at, blamed, or questioned when things did not work out. You need to remember that these things happen due to the circumstances, not because it is your entire fault or that you are being blamed for them.

There are times when the one who snapped at you is a friend of yours, or perhaps you saw doubt flash across the face of your partner. These people may have taken things out on you, but remember that you are still loved by these people. Again, it is not always about you. Hence, do not take things personally. You are still that great person that you are, who just happened to be at a certain place at a certain time, thus you received a cross remark or a hostile answer.

25 - You Are Inspiring

Live As an Excellent Example to Others

When you live as an example to others, you are not just acting out what they should all be doing; you are displaying your own modes of behavior that are natural to you and yet can be exemplary for others. This means that you show your best attitude and do things that can be good examples.

You do not only do these where there are literal audiences watching. You are also doing it for yourself, even when no one is watching. The point of this is that you make it a regular habit to be at your best behavior, with or without people seeing you. In a way, it is some kind of self-development training, where you become the kind of person who can inspire others through regular conscious action.

Soon enough, as you develop the habit of being an exemplary person, you may influence the people around you. You may inspire them to follow rules, treat others well, and respect the environment as you do. Of course, having this inspiring effect on others shall make you feel great about yourself, but more importantly, knowing that you are living your life in an exemplary way should also make you feel great.

Final Thoughts

Feeling great about yourself is not just a response to external factors that remind you how great you can be; feeling great about yourself is about recognizing what you really are and accepting it. After reading all the chapters, you now probably have a better grasp and a clearer understanding of the reality that you are indeed a great person. You just need to remember it through the powerful ways you have learned. If you noticed, each chapter is a truth about you that simply needs recognition so that you can feel great about yourself. Thus, from now on and moving forward, keep these truths in mind, and live your life in greatness!

How To Have More Courage

This book aims to help build courage in all the aspects of one's life—physically, emotionally, morally, and intellectually by acknowledging fear at its source and eventually overcoming it through understanding.

"Courage is resistance to fear, mastery of fear—not absence of fear. Courage is not the lack of fear. It is acting in spite of it." – Mark Twain

Acknowledging Fear as the Source of Courage

"Fear is essential for courage."

– John F. Murray

Since courage is simply defined as a person's willingness and ability to ultimately take action despite his fear of different things, the basic presumption is that courage requires fear in order to be exercised. It involves the existence of costs, risks, or at least a conceived threat resulting from one's action where one's ability to act in spite of them renders his act as courageous. Therefore, without fear, there can be no courage.

What is fear?

Fear is the personal sensitivity of an individual towards any harmful threat to any aspect of his well-being. It is accompanied by the physical response of avoidance associated with stress and discomfort. Thus, it can be experienced in varying degrees depending on one's ability to escape the danger he is facing. For instance, mild fear is accompanied merely by a slight degree of nervousness; sensible fear is accompanied by distress, and intense fear is accompanied by alarm and panic.

A Closer Look at Fear: The Two Faces of Fear

How fear affects a person's life depends on how he looks at it. Fear has two faces: an agent for survival or a catalyst of death.

Fear as an Agent for Survival

Through the years, fear has enabled man to contribute many inventions that played a part in human survival and development. For instance, the fear of dying from dreaded diseases such as small pox contributed to the invention and discovery of vaccines and medicines. The fear of becoming extinct from extreme weather conditions has led to the invention of stronger residential structures and appliances such as heaters and air conditioning systems in order to cope with such changes.

In these cases, man's courageousness in bringing forth ideas and discoveries which were otherwise considered eccentric or even unacceptable at that time enabled his emancipation from the dominance of nature and allowed him to ultimately conquer his fear of death.

Fear as a Catalyst of Death

On the other hand, it is when one is unable to exercise courage that he suffers from either making rash decisions or mere inaction which causes psychological illnesses such as anxiety disorders and other related ailments that may lead to deterioration in health and ultimately, death.

In fact, data from the National Institute of Mental Health indicate that nearly twenty million individuals have been found to experience such disorders the United States alone. These mental illnesses often have detrimental effects on individuals and have been found to adversely affect their work, interpersonal relationships, and their personal coping mechanisms as well. Some have been found to develop aggressive behavior and destructive routines such as drug dependency, alcoholism, and other forms of hurtful practices including murder and suicide.

It is a matter of choice.

How fear affects one's life is a matter of choice.

Identifying One's Fear

"The weeds keep multiplying in our garden, which is our mind ruled by fear. Rip them out and call them by name."
– Sylvia Browne

Individuals often make inappropriate choices in life because they allow fear to cloud their minds. In order to have a clear mind, one must first learn to identify his fear. In general, there are three types of fear: physical, emotional, and psychological fear.

Physical Fear

Physical fear is the fear of matter that is concrete or that produce tangible effects. These include fear of living things like animals, insects, fellow humans, diseases, physical pain, loss of freedom and loss or destruction of properties. It is usually felt only when one encounters the subject of fear.

Many individuals usually fear animals which are wild, violent, or poisonous like jungle animals, snakes, scorpions, and spiders. They also fear fellow humans who appear aggressive or overwhelming. In terms of diseases, they often fear illnesses which are contagious, fatal, disfiguring, or repulsive such as measles, cancer, leprosy, and other infectious skin disorders. Physical pain includes pain from violent attacks or medical procedures such as bodily injuries, incisions from surgical procedures, blood extraction, and invasive laboratory procedures. Loss of freedom is likewise a physical fear because it can be manifested in one's inability to decide, act, or move on his own such as when he enters into a relationship or engages in illegal activities which warrant imprisonment.

Emotional Fear

Emotional fear is the effect of any event that causes emotional stress or pain such as rejection, failure, loneliness, ridicule or criticism, misery, and grief. They may be induced by events like such as being turned down from a marriage proposal, losing in a competition, undergoing a financial crisis, or losing a loved one through death or separation. These fears often hinder one from advancing or moving on with his life and sometimes prevents him from taking opportunities which are otherwise good for him.

Psychological Fear

Psychological fear refers to fears created in the mind. Since the human intellect is capable of recognizing the effect of certain situations in less than seconds, fear is triggered when one does not have any experience of a circumstance he currently faces. This is because the mind cannot identify the significance of the event with respect to the effects it may produce as he has no knowledge of such in his memory. This can be also called fear of the unknown.

Recognizing the significance of certain situations enables the mind to decide or act appropriately. In other words, it allows him to exercise some degree of control. Lessening one's ability to exercise control or to at least know what he must do in specific situations trigger fear.

As soon as one identifies his fear, he can then proceed to analyze the level of fear he has. Otherwise, all these types of fear may develop into phobias if not handled appropriately.

Fear clouds the mind. Having a clear mind requires getting rid of one's fears and ridding oneself of any fears is possible only if one knows what they are.

Analyzing One's Level of Fear

"Courage is a special kind of knowledge: the knowledge of how to fear what ought to be feared and how not to fear what ought not to be feared."

– David Ben-Gurion

It is normal for a person to have a rational fear of something. On the contrary, being fearless is dangerous as one may think that he is invincible and live without necessary precautions.

Not all fears are unreasonable. Only those which have the tendency to turn into phobias can be detrimental to one's life. Thus, it is unnecessary to put a strain on one's well-being by excessive worrying about the absence of courage except in cases where the danger of fear turning into a phobia is involved. It is therefore important to distinguish between the two levels of fear: normal fears and phobias.

Normal Fears

Normal fears include childhood fears which may be outgrown such as fear of the dark and monsters, and things or events which pose real threats to one's life. Some examples of things or events which pose as real threats to one's life are crime situations such as robberies, hostage-taking, kidnapping, and murder or simply being attacked while walking down the street at night.

Normal fears do not need to be addressed with courage since they can either be outgrown or resolved without resorting to courageous acts because the individual will have a means of responding to it. For instance, the fear of darkness is always solved by providing a source of light, while the fear of crime situations can be tackled using defensive tools such as blunt weapons, guns, or sprays.

Phobias

Phobias, on the other hand, are defined as unwarranted reactions of fear towards something that is not even present or imminent. The difference between normal fears and phobias are that normal fears occur at the time when one is faced with the object of fear while phobias do not grant the individual any room for preparedness because of the lack of imminence of the object feared. Instead, phobias create a wide-ranging fear accompanied by feelings of extreme dread and panic towards the certain object or situation such that one deliberately prevents himself from encountering them even if it inhibits him from his personal advancement or induces him to change his entire lifestyle.

According to data from the National Institute of Mental Health, more than ten percent or six million Americans in the last decade experience phobias. Some of the more common phobias are animal phobias such as fear of spiders (arachnophobia), snakes (ophidiophobia), reptiles (herpetophobia), and birds (ornithophobia); situational phobias which pertain to specific events such as flying (aerophobia), climbing heights (acrophobia), being in places where one feels they cannot escape (agoraphobia), or being in enclosed spaces (claustrophobia); medical phobias which include fear of medical professionals themselves such as fear of doctors (iatrophobia) and dentists (dentophobia), fear of illness (hypochondria), germs (mysophobia), and fear of needles (trypanophobia); social phobias, spiritual phobias such as of judgment day, folklore creatures (mythophobia) and ghosts (phasmaphobia), and in recent years, nomophobia—the phobia of not having one's mobile phone resulting from an obsession to use it every minute.

An example of this difference would be having a normal fear of needles where an individual may close his eyes and squeeze a stress ball while having a blood sample drawn, while having a phobia of needles or trypanophobia would completely prevent the individual from going to a doctor for fear of being subjected to laboratory exams requiring the insertion of needles, which may ultimately lead to his death in case he has a fatal disease which was not detected due to his refusal to be examined.

To find courage in these situations, one only needs to ask himself if his fear is worth his life.

Make a stand: should one live in courage or die in fear?

Understanding One's Fear

"Fear is a question: What are you afraid of, and why? Just as the seed of health is in illness, because illness contains information, your fears are a treasure house of self-knowledge if you explore them."

– Marilyn Ferguson

Upon deciding that fear is not worth your life, one must try to overcome their fear. In order to overcome fear, the first step is to understand it. In order to understand your fear, you must identify your fear and the root cause of such fear.

Indentifying One's Fear

A person can fear many things at the same time. This may lead to future psychological disorders such as anxiety and panic disorders or even schizophrenia. Thus, it is important to know exactly what one fears in order to be able to ultimately identify and analyze the root cause of fear thus enabling a person to overcome it. This can be done by simply naming or listing down all of your fears. For instance, someone can start by recognizing that they have a fear of spiders.

The next step is to identify exactly what one fears about the certain object or situation. With respect to the example of spiders, the person shall proceed to ask themselves what exactly they fears about them. It may be their dark colors, large size, long furry legs and bodies, ability to move fast, capacity for jumping or the effects of their bites.

After identifying one's object of fear and the exact qualities which make them fearful, one may proceed to identify and analyze the root cause of his fear.

Indentifying Root Causes of Fear

The root causes of one's fear are the reasons why he fears certain objects or situations. They entail a recollection of details as to how they came to fear a certain object or situation. Through this, they will be able to focus on the proper way to handle their own fears. In general, the root causes of fear can be divided into conditioned and traumatic causes.

Conditioned Causes of Fear

Conditioned causes are those which are learned or acquired from informational sources such as reading or watching about the effects of certain situations where explicit descriptions or vivid pictures of pain are shown. In the example given on spiders, a conditioned cause may be watching a movie or television show where spiders were portrayed as threatening and dangerous creatures or seeing pictures of people suffering or dying from spider bites.

Traumatic Causes of Fear

Traumatic causes are those where an individual has suffered from a previous incident which has led him to fear the certain object or situation such as bullying, neglect, being bitten by a dog, surviving mass violence and wars, torture, natural calamities, domestic violence or maltreatment and sexual abuse. Since trauma is an emotional reaction, it is often aggravated by some circumstances surrounding the occurrence of the event which may affect one's feelings towards other things in the long run. Some of these circumstances are the unexpectedness of its occurrence, the lack of readiness on the part of the individual, the frequency of the incident, the deliberate intent in its infliction and that it occurred during childhood. They often destroy one's sense of security and accentuate one's vulnerability.

In the case of example on spiders, one may have actually suffered from a bite or has known someone who suffered or died from it.

In the United States alone, nearly three-fourths of adults or more than two hundred million individuals have experienced at least one traumatic event in their lives where around thirty million or twenty percent have developed post-traumatic stress disorders. Unfortunately, people experiencing such disorders have been found to be severely affected as they have often resorted to harmful coping mechanisms such as alcohol and drug abuse to obscure their pain. These have consequently led to aggressive behavior and decreased capacity for work and interpersonal relationships.

However, these disorders need not be experienced as long as one can face his fears and deal with them appropriately. In the end, there are only two ways of handling fear: avoiding them or facing them.

Avoiding one's fears is not necessarily an act of weakness since some fears are rational. For instance, why would one deliberately lock himself in a room full of something he fears like scorpions when he knows that there is a possible danger of being stung and dying? Avoiding exposure to harmful fears is a reasonable precaution. However, avoiding opportunities because of this fear is unreasonable. Thus, it is important to learn how to face one's fears.

The first step to overcome fear is to understand it.

Facing Fear

"What is needed, rather than running away or controlling or suppressing of any other resistance, is understanding fear; that means, watch it, learn about it, come directly into contact with it. We are to learn about fear, not how to escape from it."

– Jiddu Krishnamurti

Understanding one's fear involves more than just recognizing the reason for it. It involves facing it oneself. In order to face one's fear, one must be fully equipped as he should be before engaging in battle. He must arm himself with the proper knowledge and training before meeting his enemy. In case these prove to be insufficient, therapy or medication may also be used.

Knowledge

Learning about the object or subject of one's fear is the most important step in facing fear. This enables one to gather sufficient information on how to avoid, deal with, or even eliminate the fear. For instance, in the case of arachnophobia, knowing that there are only ten spiders which are considered as the most dangerous out of the forty thousand species that exist in the world may help him lessen his fear of spiders in general. Concentrating on the ten most dangerous species which are the brown recluse, the black widow, the Brazilian wandering spider, the Sidney funnel spider, the mouse spider, the red back spider, the wolf spider, the goliath tarantula bird-eating spider, the sac spider, and the hobo spider will enable one to recognize their appearance and pinpoint their habitat so he can prepare himself for an encounter with them in case he finds himself in their territory or finds them in his.

Training

Since training involves the use of practical skills in performing specific tasks, one must be prepared on how to handle his fears by researching on ways of eliminating them. With respect to fears related to living things such as in the example of arachnophobia, for instance, insect sprays do not usually work on spiders probably for the main reason that they are not considered as insects. Pouring seventy percent isopropyl alcohol, kerosene or anything acidic on them can damage their central nervous system and weaken them. The best way to eliminate them and ensure their death is still to whack them with a rolled up newspaper, a fly swatter or any long-handled blunt instrument that can enable one to hit them without going too near them. In this way, one is able to exercise control over the spider thus making him realize that he is more powerful than the spider thereby contributing to a decrease in his fear.

In other words, in order to overcome fear, one must always be ready with measures that would allow him to be in control of otherwise fearful events or objects. Planning ahead in terms of envisioning oneself in a fearful situation or with a fearful object may help reduce fear in the actual situation. With respect to other types of fear, one can envision himself in a plane hostage situation before his actual flight so he can think of ways of helping himself and apply them when that situation arrives. The only way to overcome fear is to be ready to face them when they surface.

Exposure

Since not all fears can be eliminated by destruction, one way of eradicating them is by actual exposure or meeting the enemy head-on. This is especially applicable to social fears, psychological fears, and harmless physical fears.

Exposure entails repeated exposure under controlled conditions. For instance, repeatedly exposing oneself to darkness may enable one to realize that nothing bad will happen in the dark thereby lessen the phobia of darkness, or constantly exposing oneself to non-venomous snakes may enable one to eliminate the fear of snakes. However, this does not mean that one should let down their defenses and be less cautious in dark environments or of venomous snakes.

Knowledge, training, and exposure are generally recommended for conditioned causes of fear. However, traumatic causes may require the professional treatment like therapy or medication.

Therapy

When one is not confident to go through the steps on their own, they may seek the help of professionals or of related interest groups through therapy. In this way, the person can develop more confidence and receive support in overcoming their fears, especially when the root cause of fear is trauma.

Yet, even without the help of a specialist, one may recover from trauma by first allowing him or herself to grieve by recalling the events or the feelings that they has been avoiding. Grief can only be known by the person feeling it. It cannot be shared by others as they can only provide sympathy. It is only by allowing oneself to grieve that they can allow themselves to heal. The process of grieving can never be hastened. It should be allowed to pass. Some people need only a short time to do so yet others spend almost their lifetime doing so.

Unless one processes the traumatic experience, it will remain in the subconscious and will continue to bother the person for a long time. Sharing the experience with others before accepting the fact that it happened is only a futile exercise, as it releases only words from one's mouth but not the emotion.

An effective way to get over trauma is to volunteer to help others face a similar situation one has gone through. Only that person can know how they can or want to be helped as a victim of a traumatic experience. By volunteering to help others and applying the method one believes would be helpful, they are also helping themselves in the process.

By doing this, he or she is able to lessen the fear he carries from the traumatic experience.

Medication

Where conscious efforts of learning, training, and exposure are not possible or when the individual is not yet ready to undergo such steps, an alternative way to eliminate fear is to use medication.

Under proper prescription, medications such as anti-depressants and other sedatives may help relieve the anxiety produced by fear. In relation to this, some studies indicate that the D-cycloserine antibiotic used in the treatment of tuberculosis may help eliminate fear together with therapies to erase memories associated with fear. However, one cannot disregard some side-effects that may be produced with prolonged use.

Thus, it is better to exert greater effort in helping oneself overcome his fears than relying on substances.

The best way to understand fear is to face it.

Overcoming Fear

"Courage is not the absence of fear, but rather the judgment that something else is more important than fear."

– Ambrose Redmoon

In order to ultimately overcome fear or at least, act in spite of it, one must find a reason to do so—a reason that weighs more than the fear itself.

As there are different types of fear, so are there different types of courage which can generally be classified according to the reasons which induce a person to exercise them— physical courage, emotional courage, moral courage, and rational courage.

In other words, each type of courage is associated with the type of fear it stems from. Thus, physical courage is an outcome of physical fear such as losing one's life in an attack; emotional courage is a result of the emotional fear of having to deal with unpleasant experiences in life; moral courage is present when an act is done in spite of the fear of the consequence of making a moral choice; and rational courage arises from the fear of the effects of the use of reasoning.

However, it is the decision to act for a value greater than that which is feared makes the exercise of courage possible. For instance, if a person values his own life more than his fear of losing it, he will protect it at all costs thereby exercising physical courage; if a person values his own happiness more than his fear of sadness he will exercise emotional courage by finding ways to experience happiness in spite of sadness; if a person values justice more than the rule of majority, he will exercise moral courage by fighting for it in spite of possible isolation; and if one values efficiency resulting from new methods more than his fear of being ridiculed for non-adherence to traditional practices, he will exercise rational courage by espousing his ideas.

Yet in all courageous acts, judgment must be used.

An act of courage is a conscious choice. As in all types of decision-making, there must be a greater motive involved.

Boosting Physical Courage

"Courage is almost a contradiction in terms. It means a strong desire to live taking the form of a readiness to die."
– G. K. Chesterton

Physical courage is often associated with typical acts of valor and honor of soldiers in wars. It generally indicates bravery in the face of physical harm or even the threat of death. In modern times, it is simply and commonly known as acting in self-defense or in defense of another.

In order to boost physical courage, one only has to put a greater value on his life or on the life of another in order to enable him to reach the maximum level where he is prepared to die so that he or another may live. This may involve thinking of the welfare of those who are dependent on him or on the other person, his personal goals or ambitions which he feels he must achieve in his lifetime or the significance of the other person in his life.

Yet, the ultimate desired result of this endeavor is to endure and triumph in the end.

In order to live, one must be ready to die.

Fostering Emotional Courage

"We are biological creatures. We are born, we live, we die. There is no transcendent purpose to existence. At best we are creatures of reason, and by using reason we can cure ourselves of emotional excess. Purged of both hope and fear, we find courage in the face of helplessness, insignificance and uncertainty."

– Jonathan Sacks

Contrary to its connotation, emotional courage does not mean expressing emotions openly regardless of the consequences. On the other hand, it involves one's openness to undergo all emotional experiences, whether positive or negative without destroying oneself in the process. As such, it requires applying the Aristotelian philosophy of choosing the middle of two extremes in order to rid oneself of emotional excesses for it is only then that one will be able to survive the emotional vicissitudes in life.

Fostering emotional courage entails accepting the reality that there will always be changes which may cause pleasant or unpleasant experiences. In doing so, one subconsciously prepares himself for the possibility of the occurrence of an unfavorable event thereby decreasing the negative impact it would have on his feelings when it arises.

Then we can say that we are ready to face life with courage.

Emotional courage is not about the denial of one's feelings. Rather, it is about tempering them.

Developing Moral Courage

"A man does what he must—in spite of personal consequences, in spite of obstacles and dangers and pressures—and that is the basis of all human morality."

– John F. Kennedy

Moral courage involves recognizing the existence of a moral situation and acting in accordance with one's moral principles or values and therefore making a moral choice. It therefore consists in doing what is right in spite of the inconvenience it may cause in one's life such as rejection, ridicule, or even isolation.

An example of this was shown by Yu Panglin, a Chinese realty and hotel magnate who, instead of leaving his sons his money as rich Chinese families would, donated his last $470 million to his charitable institutions because he was aware of the sufferings and hardships of the poor in his country. For common people, it involves making moral choices in daily activities where questions of morality may arise such as disclosing unethical or illegal business practices even if it means earning the resentment of co-workers or reporting prohibited acts such as cheating in spite of the possible ridicule from fellow students.

In order to encourage moral courage, one only has to consult his conscience.

An act of moral courage is an act of conscience.

Intensifying Rational Courage

"True courage is a result of reasoning. A brave mind is always impregnable."

– Jeremy Collier

Rational courage involves the use of reason to achieve any of these three things: discovering and promoting new ideas as well as discerning and conveying the truth, questioning one's beliefs, and thinking and overcoming one's own problems. Hence, there are three types of rational courage: intellectual, philosophical, and psychological.

Encouraging Intellectual Courage

Intellectual courage involves one's willingness to discover and promote new ideas as well as to discern and convey the truth. It also entails one's openness to take the risk of making mistakes, failing, or even being ridiculed as Copernicus (for his heliocentric theory of the universe), Gregor Mendel (for his laws of inheritance), and Albert Einstein (for his theory of relativity) have experienced in their exercise of intellectual courage.

Nevertheless, it is because of this type of courage that inventions and innovations have materialized—the benefits of which are enjoyed at present.

After all, as Albert Einstein himself once said, "What is right is not always popular and what is popular is not always right."

In order to encourage intellectual courage, one must always endeavor to seek the truth that it may be found.

Strengthening Philosophical Courage

Philosophical courage varies from the other types of courage in that it is a matter of extent more than a decision to act. In other words, courage is determined by how far one is willing to question his fundamental principles and beliefs. The farther one goes in his level of questioning, the greater philosophical courage he has. For instance, if a man is willing to question his beliefs, which he once considered unquestionable, then he is exercising a high degree of philosophical courage.

While this type of courage also entails the acceptance of the possibility of obtaining no definite answers, it nevertheless allows one to be free from biases as it broadens one's views which will eventually enable him to practice critical thinking and secure his freedom. For instance, unless one challenges his views about the existence of a god as well as his own religion, his thoughts and decisions will always be clouded by his religious beliefs which may cause his eternal slavery and hamper his development. For instance, the Catholic religion rejects the use of contraceptives as a means of birth control, and in some extreme cases, rejects birth control itself which will cause a person—particularly the woman—to be enslaved in her own body if she does not challenge or question not only this particular practice but the authority and basis upon which this belief rests as well.

However, strengthening philosophical courage entails one's willingness to let go. As T. S. Eliot writes, "Only those who risk going too far can possibly find out how far one can go." And then someday he can be free.

Improving Psychological Courage

Finally, psychological courage involves one's ability to overcome a crisis, particularly that of a diagnosed psychological problem such as a destructive or harmful habit or an unfounded anxiety. It mainly involves one's desire to reach a resolution himself as only he can direct his mind towards that which he wishes to achieve.

Improving psychological courage entails acknowledging the existence of a psychological problem. It is only then that one can move to help himself. In the words of Aristotle himself, "I count him braver who overcomes his desires than him who conquers his enemies; for the hardest victory is over self."

True courage comes with a free mind.

How to Apply Key Ideas for the Best Results?

How fear affects one's life is a matter of choice. Fear clouds the mind. Having a clear mind requires getting rid of one's fears. Getting rid of one's fears is possible only if one knows what they are.

Make a stand: should one live in courage or die in fear? The first step to overcome fear is to understand it. The best way to understand fear is to face it.

An act of courage is a conscious choice. As in all types of decision-making, there must be a greater motive involved. In order to live, one must be ready to die.

Emotional courage is not about the denial of one's feelings. Rather, it is about tempering them.

An act of moral courage is an act of conscience.

True courage comes with a free mind.

How To Heal A Broken Heart

Let's not mince words: Breaking up sucks. Regardless of who did the breaking up (i.e. you were the one who initiated *The Talk*, you were caught unaware by the breakup, or it was a mutual decision), having to say good-bye to the person with whom you've shared a special part of your life has got to be one of life's most miserable moments. And regardless of how many times you've gone through breakups, each one still stings.

If you have decided to pick up this book, good job — it means you are ready to take that first step toward healing your broken heart. In this book, you will find real-life anecdotes and advice from people who have experienced the rocky road of romance — just like you. Hopefully, their words will inspire you to pick up the pieces of your heart and focus on getting *you* back again. And hopefully, you will find in yourself the strength that you have always possessed, learn to love yourself again, enjoy being by yourself again, and finally, have the courage to open your heart someone else again.

Getting over someone is no mean feat. Luckily, you have this book to help you. The chapters are broken down into bite-size reads so you can read each one in no particular order. Let this book be your cheerleader and guide to healing your broken heart. The following chapters contain invaluable insights and action steps to take in your journey toward healing your heart. So flip to the next page and start afresh — right now!

Don't Look Back

*"Never regret yesterday. Life is in you today, and you
make your tomorrow."*

- L. Ron Hubbard

Not everyone is lucky enough to end up with the first person
they have entered into a relationship with. The first time
you end a relationship with somebody you love, it can
definitely cause you to spiral down into a pit of misery and
despair. And of course, you will go through the usual
motions of mourning the end of your relationship: bouts of
crying, listening to sad love songs, drinking until you are no
longer lucid nor reasonable enough to think and feel, and
other sorts of escapist coping mechanisms.

But here's a reality bite: What you are doing is self-
destructive. No amount of tears, alcohol, and drunken text
messages, calls, and emails will bring back the relationship
— and the person you once loved.

That said, don't waste your time poring over old mementos,
letters, emails, saved text messages, pictures, and other
reminders about your past relationship. Doing so will only
cause you more pain and heartache.

So, start afresh. Make sure to keep any reminders of your
recently deceased relationship locked away in a place that is
not easily accessible. You can even entrust those things to a
close friend or a relative whom you know has got your back.
Shares Sherry, who has been through two breakups, "I am
so thankful for my best friend, Bette. She knows that I do
not have the courage to 'clean up' concrete memories of my
exes, so she'll gather the rest of our girl friends to do it.
There was even one time when she sent back all the stuff
that my ex-boyfriend gave me to him, just to ensure that
there would be no reminders of him lying about at home."

If you must mourn the death of your relationship, allow yourself to do so at your own pace. Each person's coping mechanism is different — but what you have to be aware of is that there is a difference between grief and self-pity. Do not fall into the trap of dwelling in your sadness. If you do, you will find it more difficult to heal your broken heart.

Stop thinking and stop overanalyzing. The damage has been done; you can look at the breakup from every angle but the hard truth is, you will never be able to recover the past.

So, you may ask, what should you do now? Well, it's normal to feel bereft — after all, a person you have devoted time, effort, and love to is now gone. But what you should *not* do is beat yourself up over it. There is no use playing the blame game and stewing in feelings of bitterness and regret. Be proactive. Take time to analyze the breakup, yes, but do so with an objective mind. Find out what lessons you have learned from the relationship, and the breakup. You can do this by jotting down your thoughts in your journal or blog, talking it over with your best friend or a trusted relative, or even going to see a psychiatrist who can help you assess what happened. The most important thing in your recovery is to *not* have any regrets.

Have no regrets. Accept the fact that the relationship is over, and it is time for you to get used to your new reality.

(No) Time Heals All Wounds

"Love is like a puzzle. When you're in love, all the pieces fit, but when your heart gets broken, it takes a while to get everything back together."

- Unknown

Are you familiar with that old adage, "Time heals all wounds"? Well, in your case, one of the best ways to heal your broken heart is to have *no time* — meaning, no time to think, to regret, and to feel sad, miserable, and all those other negative emotions that come with breaking up with someone.

This piece of advice may seem like a cliché, but it is one for a reason: It's the truth. Distractions and filling up your time with activities will work in helping you heal you broken heart. The more you cocoon yourself, all alone, and hide away from the rest of the world, the harder it will be for you to heal. So be productive and be patient. Know that healing your broken heart will take time — so instead of simply waiting around for it to heal, do something *while* waiting. Opt for productive and fulfilling activities, such as:

Engaging in a new sport. Aside from the endorphin rush you'll get from working out, you will also feel a tinge of happiness and even satisfaction that you are now carving out a whole new world for yourself. This is especially true for those who have been in a long-time relationship and "share" mutual friends and acquaintances (and even family, in some cases). By doing something new, you're also creating a fresh beginning without him or her. What's more, you might even make new friends who have no idea about your previous partner — which is so liberating because there is no way they will accidentally spill something about your ex (e.g. how he or she is doing, what he or she is up to nowadays, if he or she is dating or seeing someone new).

Plus, working out can make you feel good about yourself, too! Shares Nora, who broke up with her ex-boyfriend due to "image" issues, "He said he was no longer attracted to me physically. That really crushed my self-confidence and self-esteem! For the longest time, I was so embarrassed to show myself in public. It took quite some time, but I finally mustered up the nerve to do something about my lack of self-confidence. I enrolled in the local gym, but before I did, I had to do a lot of soul-searching — I wanted to make sure that I was doing it for *me*, and not for my ex or anyone else."

Reconnecting with old friends. Now is the perfect time to hook up with old friends — and make amends with the ones whom you've neglected while you were so wrapped up in your relationship. As mentioned in the previous chapter, you should be able to pick up lessons from your heartbreak instead of dwelling in regrets and what-ifs. Perhaps one of those epiphanies is that you were so into your partner that you forgot about the other aspects in your life, which happened to Janey, an advertising executive. "I was so into Ben, my ex, that my world revolved around him and work only," she recalls. "When we broke up, I was really devastated. I felt so alone, and so ashamed because I realized that I was taking my friends for granted. And now, this guy — my ex — did the same thing to me: He took me for granted by sleeping around behind my back!" It took Janey a long time and a lot of groveling and apologizing, but she eventually won back her friends' trust. "Lesson learned: Family and friends come first. It's really true that guys come and go, so I'm putting my loved ones first — unless that guy happens to be my husband," she adds.

Taking up that language or cooking class you've wanted to for so long. Now that you have so much time on your hands, you can finally do something totally for *you*! So go ahead and take up that hobby or activity that caught your eye in the past, but which you didn't pursue because you were too busy with "other" things. Embrace the fact that now you are totally free to do whatever you want (as long as you are not hurting anyone else, of course) and that your actions are not accountable to anyone except yourself. Rejoice in your newfound singlehood — it is one of the best feelings in the world!

Going on trips with friends and/or family. Listen to this story from Leslie, who recently broke up with her ex-fiancé. "The breakup was a long time coming," she remembers. "Yet, it was perfect timing that when we broke up — technically, it was a mutual decision, but not really on my part because deep down, I was still hoping that we would get back together — I had a planned beach trip with my friends the day after. I broke the news to them then, and they made sure that I was okay the entire time. On my end, I tried my best not to be wet blanket since we were also celebrating two of my friends' birthdays." She adds with a chuckle, "It was a good thing that I had already paid the deposit ahead of time — I was so tempted to bail from the trip and just hole up in my room!"

Take a cue from Leslie and get your mind off your devastation with a change of scenery. It will do you a whole lot of good to get away for a while, especially if you will be surrounded by your support system. You can also go on a solo trip if you are more comfortable with that idea, but just make sure that you won't waste the entire trip by hibernating in your hotel room — go out, have fun, take long walks, do some sight-seeing, and make an effort to meet new people and make new friends so you are not spiraling down even further into the pit of depression.

The possibilities of filling up your social calendar are endless! And if you are stuck without ideas, your friends and family are there to help you out. You simply need to reach out to them.

"When I broke up with my ex, I hid from the rest of the world," recalls Paula, a home-based graphic and web designer. "My friends let me be for a couple of days, then they showed up and told me we were going out clubbing. They got me all dolled up and it felt really good. They really looked out for me — I had a few drinks, but just enough to give me a buzz. Afterward, they made sure I was so occupied with so many things that I didn't have the time and energy to feel sad. Those were good distractions — happy, positive ones. They kept me from going insane with grief."

The bottom line is: Channel your energies toward positive things. Keep your mind and body busy and refocus your effort, time, and attention elsewhere. At this point in your life, it is important to have your loved ones around you. Let them help you mend your broken heart. Do not be afraid to seek their help. Know that you are not alone in the process of healing your heart.

Make sure that you have your support system with you as you go through this tough time in your life. You will need them to rally around you and cheer you on as move toward the next phase in your life.

You Are Not Broken — Just Your Heart

"I don't know why they call it heartbreak. It feels like every other part of my body is broken, too."

- Anonymous

It's easy to think that there is something wrong with you just because you got dumped or broke up with your significant other, think again. There is *nothing* wrong with you!

Stop berating yourself for being the cause of the breakup — and consequently the cause of your broken heart. Remember, it takes two to tango, and that means that the breakup (regardless of who initiated it) stemmed from issues between you two — *not* because you are not capable of loving, or because somehow, your way of loving someone else is "defective."

Another thing: Do not think that your newfound single status means that you are a lesser human being. You don't need anyone to make you happy or whole. That kind of thinking will make you depressed *and* desperate, and you'll be jumping from one relationship to another, seeking approval from your partner all the time.

Former US First Lady Eleanor Roosevelt once said, "No one can make you feel inferior without your consent." Chew on this. If you let someone else have that much power over you, to the point that you need his or her validation to make you feel that you are a person of worth, then you are not being true to yourself. It is *your* job and *your* responsibility to find and create your own happiness, and to tell yourself that you *are* a person of worth. You do not need anyone else to convince you of that.

Look around you. There are so many people who love and care for you. Why should the breakup make you feel less of a person? Just because one relationship didn't work out, you should not think that you do not deserve to be loved romantically again. If you keep thinking this way, then you are letting not just your heart, but your entire being, to be broken.

Draw strength and inspiration from your church. Join support groups — surely, there is one in your neighborhood that talks about self-affirmation and loving yourself. Read inspirational books — these are proof that you are not alone in your heartache, that you have the power within you to heal your broken heart and make yourself feel "whole" again. Simply put, *you* have the power to make yourself believe that you are worthy — no one else can.

Stay away from people who will only look at you with pity in their eyes. Even though they *might* mean well, chances are, their pity will make you feel bad about yourself. Surround yourself with positive people, those who constantly remind you that their lives and the world are so much better with *you* in it. But do not use these people as a crutch. In the end, you are responsible for filling that "void" you are feeling right now with the loss of someone important in your life — and not through relying on another person (i.e. entering into another relationship), but discovering your joy and happiness on your own as a single person.

Remember that you are a strong person. You are responsible for your own happiness. You do not need another person to make you whole, because you are whole by yourself already.

Keep Your Focus

"Pain is inevitable. Suffering is optional."

- M. Kathleen Casey

In your journey toward healing, it is inevitable that you will experience bumps and obstacles that may lead you to slide back to self-pity and depression. You will have days when you will doubt if you are truly okay, when your insecurities will come rushing back full force to the surface, and you will be tempted to crawl back into that hole you just came out of.

Relax! Those experiences are normal. What matters is that you are aware that these things *will* happen, and that you have the emotional arsenal to keep yourself in check — and on track toward fully mending your broken heart.

So keep your focus and stay away from these self-destructive behaviors:

Going on the rebound. As mentioned in previous chapters, jumping into another relationship so soon after you have just broken up with someone is not advisable. Take pity on yourself and the other person. You are only using him or her to distract you from your pain — and not in a good way. What you need to do is to detach yourself from the dating scene, and concentrate on being happy and finding fulfillment on your own.

Not eating, or eating too much. There are people who turn to food when they're down, and there are also those who refuse to eat at all. Find a balance. If you find yourself eating too much, put a stop to it. Know that you can do it! You are not helpless against your depression and heartache — you are stronger than that. On the other hand, if you find that you have no appetite, make sure that you take light snacks and drink water throughout the day to compensate for those "real" meals.

Hibernating. Don't close yourself off from the rest of the world. Your family and friends will worry, and they want to spend time with you! Make an effort to go out and meet with them, even if it's only just once a week. "They will definitely cheer you up and help you focus on your healing process," says Amy, who managed to overcome her depression after a particularly nasty divorce.

Letting your performance at work slide. Don't let your breakup affect your job. Keep your professionalism intact and make it a point to pour your heart and soul into being a rockstar at work. You have no distractions (i.e. your ex) anymore, so now you can go full-force into being the best at work!

Turning to alcohol and drugs to help you get through the pain. By doing this, you are not hurting your ex, but yourself and the people who love you. Here is a piece of tough love from Grant, who has been through it. "When I broke up with my ex, I started partying hard, drinking hard, doing drugs, sleeping with any girl who was willing. That was totally unlike me," he shares. "Then, one day, my friends staged an intervention. They told me that I was being a jerk and that no amount of partying, alcohol, drugs, and women would help me get back together with my ex-girlfriend." What's worse, Grant says, is that his friends drilled this thought into his head: "She broke up with me and was moving on with her life, while I was stuck in this hell. My best friend actually told me, 'Dude, she wouldn't care what happens to you now. She may feel a little sad, but her world won't stop for you. So why are you letting your world stop for *her*?' Boy, was that a gigantic wake-up call!"

People say that living well is the best revenge. It may sound a little mercenary, but it's true. You don't really have to think about living well as *revenge* per se, but you should have the mindset that living well is your way of showing the world *and* yourself that you will survive in the midst of your heartache. Believe in yourself!

Upon the advice of her shrink, Tess found out a good way to help lift her spirits up when she was trying to heal her broken heart. She got out her journal and started listing down her strengths. When she ran out of ideas, she turned to her friends and family to help her fill up the list. "I take it out every so often whenever I have the blues," she says. "There are still days when I feel bleak, when I feel insecure, when I doubt myself, but reading the list again reminds me of everything I should be thankful for, and what makes me special."

You can also get in touch with your spiritual side, which Katie did. After breaking up with her ex-boyfriend, Katie found herself going to church more often. She's still not a "hardcore" Catholic, but she says that visiting church on her own helped her find serenity amidst the chaos of her heartbreak. "My best friend forwarded me the Serenity Prayer, and I always pray it whenever I feel like breaking down."

The Serenity Prayer reads:

God, grant me the serenity to accept the things I cannot change; the courage to change the things I can; and the wisdom to know the difference.

Living one day at a time; enjoying one moment at a time; accepting hardships as the pathway to peace; taking, as He did, this sinful world as it is, not as I would have it; trusting that He will make all things right if I surrender to His will; that I may be reasonably happy in this life and supremely happy with Him forever in the next. Amen.

Learn to love yourself again. Keep your list of strengths handy. Take it out whenever you feel yourself sliding back into that abyss of self-pity and insecurity.

Face And Fight; Do Not Take Flight

"There are things that we don't want to happen but have to accept, things we don't want to know but have to learn, and people we can't live without but have to let go."

- Unknown

People are inherently wired to fight or flight when faced with a crisis. For most of those who are reeling from a broken relationship, they tend to take the easy way out by escaping or taking flight — be it going on the rebound, drinking themselves to oblivion, and not manning up to the issues that are related to the breakup. It's an understandable and normal reaction, but it's not a healthy one.

According to psychologists and relationship experts, one of the healthiest and best ways to mend a broken heart is to face the pain head-on. Do not give in to the urge to flee, to jump into another relationship just because you are scared of being alone. If you still love your ex and you know that you are not yet ready to give your heart to another person, then spare yourself and the other another round of heartbreak. Do not give in to your loneliness and get caught up in another relationship right away, as it will only end disastrously. This was one lesson that Allan learned the hard way. "When my ex-girlfriend broke up with me, my self-confidence really plummeted," he shares. "There was this girl, Tina, who I knew always had a thing for me. I was on the rebound, and I was lonely and insecure, and she was ready and willing. We ended up together, until one day, I realized that I was with her for all the wrong reasons. Boy, ending things with her was really tough — and it made me even more depressed."

Breakups can make you feel that you are not lovable enough. It's a normal reaction, but you shouldn't act on that feeling. What you should always keep in mind is that the relationship didn't work out because of the issues both of you faced as a couple — it is not a case of "It's not you, it's me," or "It's not me, it's you." It is *both* of you, but since he or she is not around anymore, then *you* will have to face your issues on your own — so that the next time you will be entering into a relationship, you are wiser and know better.

You can try to examine what went wrong in the relationship from all angles on your own, but it is better to get the input of your friends (or, if you can afford it, a professional therapist) and family. They may be able to spot some things that you can't, since it is impossible for you to be 100 percent objective. It's okay to be in denial at first — after all, healing your broken heart is similar to grieving and its stages (denial, anger, bargaining, depression, and acceptance). However, at one point, you must summon the courage to admit where *you* went wrong. As Zane says, "It hurt me to admit it, but I wasn't 100 percent into the relationship, and that's why my ex-girlfriend, Sasha, broke up with me. I was just too darn proud to admit it then." Now, Zane says, he knows better and that the next time he has a girlfriend, he'll make sure that he is really willing to commit. "It wouldn't be fair to me and the girl if I am not dedicated to making the relationship work."

Jasmine, who became a single mom at the age of 18, has also had her share of heartaches. It wasn't until she began seeing a therapist that she was able to fully understand why all her previous relationships failed. "I was insecure that being a single mom meant my 'market value' was down, that no guy was ever going to want me, so I would always hook up with any guy who showed interest in me," she admits. "I became 'easy,' and that really made my friends and family mad. They said I was being self-destructive. At first, I was in denial, but after the fourth breakup, I finally saw the light."

Even if you haven't had a string of heartaches like Jasmine, you might still be able to figure out a pattern among your relationships — past and present. And understand that working out your issues will take time, so be patient. Don't let your frustration get the better of you — take it one day at a time, and one step at a time. Soon, your broken heart will be fully healed.

Every day, look in the mirror and tell yourself, "I am strong. I will get through this. I will survive, and even thrive."

Get A Move On

"If someone you love hurts you, cry a river, build a bridge, and get over it."

- Unknown

To truly mend your broken heart, you need to come to terms with the breakup — and by that, it means you need closure. There are some people who are able to get past heartaches without closure, but more often than not, people need that final "period" to finally get past their heartbreak.

People have different ways of closure, and just like working out your relationship and personal issues, know that it will take time and effort. Your kind of closure may come in the form of having that final talk with your ex, seeing your ex with somebody else, or finally letting go of the anger and bitterness in your heart and forgiving your ex — *and* yourself.

If you must, pour out all your painful thoughts and feelings of anger and sadness on a piece of paper, or type them all out in your blog, then promptly delete the post or burn the paper immediately. It's a cathartic way to exorcise your emotional demons, and finally say good-bye to your heartache.

Some people cannot forgive and forget; they can only forgive, but not forget. If you fall into the latter category, it's okay — what matters is that you are able to forgive and move on. Perhaps the most important point in healing your broken heart is finding hope and having faith that you *are* enough, and that you will love again.

For Marc, who admits to having a lot of pride, it took him almost a year before he could really say that he wishes his ex well. "As far as I know, she's still not seeing anyone. We're not friends; we don't keep in touch. But for the longest time, we both stayed away from each other because we were too mad. But then, I don't know, I guess holding on to anger was just too much of an effort. It's quite draining. After I worked out my personal issues, I decided to reach out and greet her a happy new year. She returned the greeting, and from then on, we're cool," he says. "We'll never be friends like we were before we became a couple, but at least I know that we don't have any more ill feelings toward each other."

Don't lose hope. Learn to forgive yourself. Believe that you *will* find love again — and that you are ready and brave enough to face that eventuality when it happens.

How to Apply What You've Learned

If you have finished reading the chapters and have reached this part of the book, congratulations! You are now equipped with the knowledge and insight to heal your broken heart.

As hard as it is, believe that you have the strength and grace in you to let go of the resentment and bitterness accompanying your broken heart. Only by forgiving yourself and your ex, and coming to terms with your relationship, will you be able to get past your broken heart.

Here is a quick summary of the chapters and key steps to take toward healing your broken heart:

1. Let go of the past. Do not dwell on the what-ifs. Do not worry about the future as well. Live in the present, and begin healing your broken heart by acknowledging the pain.

2. Fill your time with positive activities that make you happy. Do rewarding, fulfilling things such as going on trips with friends and family, volunteering for a cause, exercising and working out, and the like. Stay away from self-destructive behaviors such as binge drinking, partying, and substance abuse.

3. Never, ever think that you are not enough, that you are not a lovable human being. You are capable of love and being loved. Your broken heart does not mean that you are a failure and that you made a mistake. Look at your relationship as an important life lesson that will make you a wiser, better, and stronger person.

4. Have constant reminders of your goal, which is to heal your broken heart. Don't let obstacles and frustrations get in your way. Don't allow these setbacks deter you from being 100 percent okay again.

5. Figure out your personal issues and work through them. Don't escape your problems and sadness with masochistic and self-destructive activities. Know that you are strong and capable of healing your broken heart.

6. You will never be able to move past your heartbreak if you do not have closure. Seek closure and be patient — it will come, sooner or later. Finally, believe that you will find love again.

How To Live In The Moment

Benjamin Franklin once said, "Dost thou love life? Then do not squander time, for that's the stuff life is made of."

How right he is. Our lives are always tied to the tiers: past, present, and future. Unfortunately, many people are either hung up on the past they can no longer have, or anxious of the future that is still to come. Too few of us really live in the present. We squander the time meant for the present on the past and future.

It's a corporate world we live in, with money and numbers zigzagging around our atmosphere. We're hardly living, and merely existing. It doesn't help either that our film industry has sought to keep producing zombie films. Perhaps the zombies are us?

This book will show you some ideas and ways on how you can train yourself to live in the present, to actually live in the now. You will learn ways to unclutter your thoughts, to stand still but fulfilled in a busy world, and to take charge of your life. So, brace yourself, your life is about to change.

Meditate

"To a mind that is still, the whole universe surrenders."

– Lao Tzu

Maybe every time you've read this word, you've imagined bald monks sitting cross-legged for hours or even days in complete silence, with their eyes closed, so still you aren't sure that they're still breathing. You're not far off, as meditation is not just a new exercise technique. It's been around for centuries and Buddhist monks have used this. How else do you think they transcend over problems like rent or the next episode on the lives of the Kardashians?

From Siddhartha Gautama's serious meditation techniques since 500 BC, this practice of silence in a still pose has spread from the East to the West slowly. This has now become one of the techniques people use to give themselves a sense of peace in a very stressful world.

Where does living in the moment fit into this? You live in an information age where everything you need is at the tip of your fingers, at the other end of the line, and at the click of a button. With the media and internet giving you everything you could want in the blink of an eye, everything else is also speeding up.

Consider this: you need to get to work within 15 minutes. The files need to be delivered today. You need to get married before you hit your 30's. You finished a college degree so that you could proceed to law. Everything is expected to be done at the snap of a finger. You're always told to think an hour from now, to consider your future, to think fifty years from now so often that you're almost dizzy from the assault of too much hustle and bustle. Do you even have time to breath?

Relax. Meditate. Take a break from your bustling day—even just an hour—to meditate. A professor at Harvard Medical School, Dr. Herbert Benson, discovered that meditation helps prevent the effects of the sympathetic nervous system, which tells the human body to react immediately in conflicts. This is exactly the reason why people tend to get easily stressed when there are deadlines to finish and expectations to fulfill.

Meditation lowers your blood pressure. It lowers chances of phantom pains (and real aches). It also helps you breathe better. It helps unclutter your mind. Working every day, around the clock with no breathing time will only drive you to more stress and an early grave. Everything will pass you by, and before you know it, you're facing the next day, or the next year.

Find a spot at home, or go to a yoga class, and just be still for a while. Breathe, and stop thinking of your boss. Give this time to yourself—and yourself alone. Take a moment to re-organize your thoughts. Meditate and just still your mind in a busy world.

Take a Hike

"It's the little things that are vital. Little things make big things happen."

- John Wooden

Life is short. Don't let it pass you by without noticing what's around you. Remember that film about a guy who had a magical remote? He could put subtitles, fast word, and rewind things. The problem was he pressed the fast-word button far too many times that he jumped to the future, but was on auto-pilot in the present.

Don't be that guy. Don't be on auto-pilot. Take the time to notice your surroundings. When was the last time you looked at your garden and actually looked at the roses your wife planted? Have you ever seen how the sun looked like when it first broke through the clouds? Or were you too busy running after the bus?

Here's a suggestion: take a hike. No, seriously and literally, take a hike, preferably a long one. Not only is it a form of exercise, it's also good for your blood sugar level. Tel Aviv University has done studies that reveal how walks can be good for your back.

Undoubtedly, 24/7 sitting on a chair in a cubicle will never be good for your health, so take some time to stretch your legs and walk. You can discover so many things during long walks.

When you hike or walk up and down your street, take the time to notice the little things like your neighbors who play with their puppy on a good day, the big tree at the end of the block, or even something as mundane as the color of your rooftop. When you learn to notice these little things, you also learn to appreciate that life isn't all about the numbers or money. Money might get you a gold coffin, but it certainly won't cry for you or miss you when you're gone.

What do you do when you take a long walk to not look like a creeper or a stranger person stalking the streets? Talk to the people. Make small talk with a neighbor trimming bushes. Pat a cat on the head. Walk your dog. Let *other people* pat your pet on the head. Drink a warm cup of coffee. Drink it— don't chug it down like it's a pill!

Look around you and be in the moment because when this moment passes, you can never get it back. You might never have been absent at work, but you sure might not ever have been present, mentally and physically in your family gatherings or neighborhood BBQ.

Turn It Off

"It has become appallingly obvious that our technology has exceeded our humanity."

– Albert Einstein

It is common knowledge that Albert Einstein was a genius. He was so smart that he saw how our technology would one day run almost everything in our lives—from birth to death. Without a doubt, technology has made the world so much bigger and smaller at the same time. Technology has its advantages and disadvantages, but how you can you tell when you're already suffering from the latter?

It's when you live for the YouTube channels you subscribe to, the Facebook status of your friends, the next episode of your favorite daytime soap, or even the blow-by-blow tweets of your favorite sports game.

They may seem important to you, but you can't live off them. Yes, Facebook shows some important news bits every now and then, and the FIBA game isn't every month, but do you need to check your FB live feed every other minute? Do you really need to upload every picture you take of yourself on Instagram and tag everyone you know?

Take a break and turn off your TV. Turn off your computer, and stop checking your phone every second. A new research study from the University of Gothenburg, Sweden reinforces the fact that the artificial lighting and ultraviolet light from technological devices causes more stress and fatigue. Aside from tying your life to other people's buzz, your health gets affected, too!

Ray Bradury's novel *Fahrenheit 451* reveals a dystopian era where books are burned and people live off of and for their TV shows. Life doesn't revolve around boxes of media alone.

Don't let what other people had for lunch tie you down to the computer for hours.

Look around you. Get out of the house. Leave your laptop at home. If you want to communicate with a friend, give her a call. Go to her house and have a chat. Social media is not a substitute for actual interaction. TV shows are not a substitute for the kind of life you want to live.

Every once in a while, turn off the TV or the computer. Stop reading how other people are living their lives and start living yours! The world is so much bigger than a 21-inch screen.

Smile and Laugh More

"A smile is a curve that sets everything straight."

– Phyllis Diller

It's a reaction. It should be a reflex, but more and more people are finding less and less reasons to smile. Would you smile if you knew you only had one day left to finish a report? Would you smile, thinking constantly of the mortgage or the student loans you have yet to pay off?

Well, those problems won't go away if you frown. They won't go away either when you smile, but when you do stretch those facial muscles in a curve, you become happier. That's right: A smile isn't just an outward manifestation of happiness. Smiling can *cause* joy. When you stretch the zygomatic major (the facial muscle needed to smile), your brain gets told, "You're happy about something."

And laughter? Institutes around the world have employed techniques on laughter yoga—strategies to induce laughter. Your body won't be able to tell the difference between real and fake laughter, which means that the benefits you get when you genuinely laugh will be the same as laughter induced by laughter yoga techniques. Also, like your smile, fake laughter can cause you to laugh genuinely. You'll eventually find something to laugh about—the fact that you're forcing yourself to laugh is funny enough.

Research conducted in Bangalore, India, revealed that laughter lowers your blood pressure and stress levels. When you live in a world where you experience stress on a daily level, smiling and laughing can help you keep yourself sane.

Everyone has problems. You have problems that may be emotional, physical, or financial. Deal with these problems with a frown and you'll just get more stressed. Deal with them with a smile and occasional laughter and you'll feel better. Not only will it lighten your mood, it'll also make you more than ready to deal with problems.

Smile and laugh some more. It might not lessen the problems, but it will lighten the stress. Sometimes, when you can't beat the problem, the only thing you can do is to give yourself more strength to deal with it. Sometimes, it's how you react to the problem that makes a difference. Someone who smiles despite the problems is bound to be more productive than someone who hardly ever smiles.

A smile and laughter can go a long way in making you feel better. Problems don't go away with a frown, but they do feel lighter and easier to deal with when you smile. You only live once. Don't spend most of your days with a frown.

Be Kind

"What wisdom can you find that is greater than kindness?"
– Jean Jacques Rousseau

It's never overrated to be kind to people, even strangers. When you live in the moment, you also remember that you're not the only one living in the world. After being stuck in a rat race, you remember that not everyone in the world is in a competition with you.

Start doing things for people without being told to do so. Give them a random gift. Praise them when they do a job well done. Help them when they can't seem to get the door open. Be kind to people who need help. They will either look suspiciously at you or thank you, but what do you have to lose?

They might not know your name, they might even forget your face, but they will never forget that someone did something good to them without looking forward to a reward. Altruism is beautiful but dying word, yet we owe so much to people who have shown us genuine kindness.

Have you seen the film about a boy who, instead of letting people pay him back for the kindness he does, tells them to "pay it forward" instead? Don't just be kind to those who were kind to you. That grumpy neighbor across your house? Tell him his garden's nice or wave and smile a good morning to him. Maybe he didn't grow up with a lot of kind people. Maybe you could change that for him.

Sonja Lyubomirsky, Ph.D., a professor of psychology at the University of California, Riverside, after conducting studies and research, said that acts of kindness make people feel happier—both the doer and receiver of the act. When you're kind to people, chances are, you'll have a better day.

Scientifically, when you act kindly towards someone, you feel a sense of "warmth," which is produced by a hormone, oxytocin. Oxytocin, in turn, produces nitric oxide, which protects your heart by lowering the blood pressure.

You live in this world, but you're not the only one. Look around you and appreciate the people in your vicinity. What lives are they living? Have you made an impact on their lives, or do you sit behind a computer all day, not even noticing the proverbial old woman trying to cross the street?

Helping others can make you feel better. It can also gain you new friends and acquaintances. Remember that you share this world with a million others. How many have you helped today?

Be Thankful

"What if you woke up today with only the things you thanked God for yesterday?"

– Anonymous

Ask and you shall receive. The problem is most of us just kept on asking, and we keep on forgetting to thank. No matter what your religion is or what you believe in, you can never say thank you enough. What if all you've been doing the whole day was complaining how your wife couldn't cook well, or how your father never listens to you? You wake up the next day and everything you were never thankful for disappeared. What would you have left?

You're only mortal and you live on borrowed time. You know that death is certain, but you don't know how and when you'll die. You do know each moment you have still alive should never be wasted.

When was the last time you thanked your parents, teachers, children, or your grandparents? Did you say thank you to the cashier who has bags under her eyes? Maybe she's working three jobs to put food on the table. Your simple thank-you could make her feel better. It would also make her feel that her efforts, no matter how small, are appreciated.

You know that every minute of your life is measured. Every word you say has weight. You hold a conference and you're paid for your time and your words, but how much time do you spend saying, "Thank you," and mean it?

Do you wonder why the title of this section is "Be Thankful" and not "Be Grateful"? Being grateful is a feeling—it's an emotion for when you feel warm and fuzzy inside because someone helped or praised you. Being thankful is more of an action. It means that when you feel grateful, you say it—through words or deeds.

What do you have to be thankful for? Look beyond your debts and the bills. You have a family that loves you. You have people who rely on you. You have people who appreciate you. You could be thankful for the tiny baby who cries every time you're away because she needs you. You should be thankful for the chance to walk to work instead of being in a wheelchair. You would certainly be thankful for a day spent recovering in a hospital if it meant you still have your life ahead of you. This day alone should be enough to be thankful for. Not everyone can wake up from sleep. Some fade away before the sun rises.

Appreciate each moment and be thankful for each day given to you because yesterday is gone and tomorrow might never come.

Wait Wisely

"Don't spend time beating on a wall, hoping to transform it into a door."

– Coco Chanel

No truer words have ever been spoken by the great Coco Chanel. In a fast-paced world, who likes to wait? The corporate world doesn't. Justice doesn't. The activists who want change certainly don't. The guy waiting 15 minutes for his pizza absolutely won't, but life rarely gives you what you want. It'll give you apples if you wanted lemons.

Imagine yourself rushing to work. It's barely 8 a.m. and you're stuck in the subway waiting for the next train, which will be an hour from now. What do you usually do? Most likely, you'll be tapping your shoes on the pavement, looking around at the people who are in as much of a hurry as you, looking at your watch every two minutes, and checking your phone for a call or text. Basically, you're going to spend the hour waiting for your train anxious and nervous.

So what should you do? If it's not in your power to speed up the train, then you should learn to wait wisely. They say that time flies by when you're having fun. The opposite is true. When you're not having fun, time seems to slow down. The more you wait anxiously for the train to arrive, the slower time seems to be running.

Distract yourself. Do something while you wait. Is there a book you've been meaning to read, but never had the time? Bring that book or read it on your phone. You could already be way into the climax when you hear the train coming in.

Listen to music or sing a song. You don't have to tune out the whole world, but people who listen to music while waiting are more relaxed and less anxious. If you don't have a set of earphones, you can hum a tune under your breath. Try to remember the lyrics of your favorite song.

Try to solve a puzzle. Solving the Rubik's cube is all the rage. Even if you're not a genius, you can bring a small cube with you and use it to distract yourself. It will give you a sense of focus and maybe one of these days you can actually solve it.

If you don't do any of these things, then just simply look around you and observe people. Why is that old woman beside you traveling alone? Who is she going to meet? How old do you think that girl is? What are her dreams and ambitions?

Divert the focus away from yourself and look at the world around you. There are actually many things you might not have noticed before. You can't do anything about the wait, but you can do something while waiting.

Try Something New

"When was the last time you did something for the first time?"

– Anonymous

The world is a constantly changing place. People change. Ideas change. So why should you be stuck doing something over and over again, without progress? Once in a while you get stuck in a rut and you see yourself doing the same routine for the next ten years. Do you seriously want to live that way?

When was the last time you did something for the first time? When was the last time you tried something new? When you were in high school? When you had your first job? Even machines have to be oiled once in a while to keep them functional. Doing something new—a break from the mundane—is your fuel.

Have you been working a nine-to-five job for 15 years? Well, haven't you ever thought of using all your business know-how to run your own business? It's the 21st century, and the peak of online e-commerce is still on the rise. You don't need to have a building to get into business.

Do something you've been afraid of doing for a long time. Go skydiving! Go surfing! Once in a while, do something that makes your heart race. Do something spectacularly amazing that you'll never forget for as long as you live. Swim the dolphins and scale Mt. Everest. It's a short life. Don't let the good things pass you by.

Perform in front of a large crowd. You don't think you have a good voice or killer dance moves? Pfft. Who cares? They're not paying you, anyway. Go to a karaoke place and blast eardrums off with your own rendition of a rock song or serenade people in the streets with a musical instrument you know how to play. The adrenaline you will feel performing on stage will be unforgettable. It's only once anyway. Make the most of it.

Join an organization and volunteer! You've been handed many blessings in life. It's time to give some to others. You might be able to go to places you didn't know exist and meet people you didn't think could be friends. You don't get any pay, but the smiles of those you helped will be more than worth the money you didn't make.

Cook or bake something. The oven or the stove might seem daunting, but you can never say you've done it all until you've cooked one edible meal. It doesn't have to be something unique or expensive. Just a simple bacon-and-eggs dish or a small cake can make you feel accomplished.

The world is huge and there are still so many things you can try. Don't limit yourself to what you've been doing for so many years. Try something new and discover new talents you never thought you had.

Travel

"Not all those who wander are lost."

– J. R. R. Tolkien

Have you caught yourself looking wistfully at pictures of Rome, Thailand, or Alaska? Whether or not you're prepared to admit it, you have been bitten by the travel bug. Most people have.

The 2013 film loosely based on a short story of the same title, *The Secret Life of Walter Mitty* tells us that wanderlust is very real, once it has taken ahold of you. Walter Mitty might have traveled to do his job, but he experienced so many things that his job seemed trivial compared to what he had done: survived a close call of a volcanic eruption, got into a "shark-fight," traveled across foreign lands on a shipping vessel, bike, and skateboard, not to mention the trek up the Himalayas. He did all these after 15 years of working in a small, dim-lighted room developing negatives for the magazine.

Although Walter Mitty is a figment of imagination, Liz Carlson certainly isn't. An English teacher in Spain who returned to D.C. to work a nine-to-five job suddenly realized that the life she wanted to live was not found in lone cubicles and quarterly meetings. She saved up and traveled the world, writing and blogging.

She's certainly not the only one. Ying Tey backpacked the world after her mother's death, realizing that life really is short and living in a routine-run box was only going to make hers shorter.

Travel is one the greatest things you can do in life. It's not the same as taking a vacation, though. Vacation is for relaxation. Traveling takes some effort. When you travel, you don't get away from your boss, your deadlines, or your heartaches. Travel is getting away *into* a new place and discovering a new culture. You travel for the sake of traveling.

It doesn't have to be an expensive trip. A long road trip to the next state can be your first genuine travel experience. A ferry ride to a small island can be a simple travel.

You've probably experienced how suffocating a neck tie can be, or how difficult it is to wear high heels every day. Sometimes, you just have to trade the neck tie for a camera dangling around your neck, and your heels for a pair of comfy sneakers.

Travel is a rewarding experience where you can challenge yourself and be you in a new place. You can reinvent yourself and do things you couldn't do before in your hometown. When you travel, you don't just discover new places and meet new people, you meet yourself as well.

Dream Awake

"'What if I fall?' Oh, but my darling, what if you fly?"

–Erin Hanson

You don't have to read a long list of people like Walt Disney, Steve Jobbs, or J. K. Rowling to know that these people took a leap of faith. They dreamt and acted on it. They didn't give up. They lived the life they wanted, despite hundreds of people telling them they couldn't do it.

They're obviously not the only ones with dreams. Most people have dreams. From having a family of four to being a rockstar, dreams vary from person to person. The question is, do you do all you can to reach your dreams?

If you're stuck in a job you don't like, ask yourself why you don't like your job and how you got into that job in the first place? Most people flock towards a job for the paycheck, benefits, and fame. Those things will not keep you happy for long. You're not born into the world merely to survive, but to live.

If you live for money, you're not going to last long. Why do you think most people are depressed and suicidal? If you're holding on to a job only because you're afraid to go fulfill your dreams because you fear rejection, unemployment, insecurity, or pressure from family or friends, do remember the people mentioned in the first line of this chapter.

J. K. Rowling was a divorcee with young children. She wrote a story and asked several publishers for the chance to have it printed. Of course, no one took her seriously. It was too mature for children and too immature for adults. She didn't stop asking and looking for a publisher who would give her a chance, until one took a chance on her, and the rest, as you know, is history.

Rowling didn't sit and mope all day. She didn't sleep all day either. Whatever her dreams were, she was awake enough to make them come true. Do you have a dream? A cause you've always wanted to live for? If you say that it's too difficult, too impossible, too uncertain to do, then don't ever hope to fulfill it. You're the only one who can reach your dreams, but you have to be awake to do it.

A writer, Holly Lisle, once said, "One day you'll wake up and discover that the part of yourself that knew how to dream— and how to fly—has died, and that you are forever after bound to the ground, with only the memory that you once had wings. Every dreamer pays a price. But so does everyone who fears to dream."

Dreaming isn't only for those who are dead to their world and stuck in a realm of their own making. If you want to sing for a living, then by all means, do everything in your power to make that dream real. Your dream won't come true today, but it will start happening right now.

How to Apply Key Ideas for the Best Results?

How should you live your life right now? How do you live in the moment? Before you go and travel to Asia, sit down and think about all the things you've read. This world is always on the go, and you are stuck in a hamster's wheel, running and running but always in the same place.

Make a checklist of the things you've done and want to do. Follow the steps in the book and integrate them in your day to day activities.

Meditate either at home or in a studio. Set aside a specific schedule for a full meditation time. Also, when you're stressed at work, set aside at most 30 minutes to just sit down, close your eyes, and relax. Regular meditation will help loosen muscles and heavy shoulders.

Take a hike in your neighborhood or just a small walk in your own garden. Take things slowly and notice the little things. Walk around your office during lunch break and just observe people. Seeing how busy other people are will give you an insight into how *you* are when you're in the rat race.

Don't use the TV or the internet once in a while. Don't spend all of Saturday watching movies back to back. Stop waiting for the live feed of your friends' posts every minute. Talk to people face to face and listen to the conversations happening right in your vicinity.

Smile and laugh, even just a little bit every now and then. Find something good to brighten your day or listen to upbeat or uplifting songs!

Be kind to people you meet—whether it's the cafeteria lady or the janitor. Make someone else's day.

Give thanks to another day for you to correct your mistakes and do more good work for others.

Bring a puzzle, a book, or a headset while waiting for the bus or waiting in line. Look at the people around you and try to strike up conversations with fellow passengers.

Try something new! Adopt a pet or get a new haircut. It's time to freshen up and do some changes.

Travel and learn. Discover things you never thought existed, and come home with a trunk full of memories.

Sit down and listen to your thoughts. What do you really want to do in life? What do you want to use your skills and talents for? Don't get carried away with imagining a successful future just yet. You won't reach success if you don't start now. Johann Wolfgang von Goethe sums it up best saying, "Nothing is worth more than this day." Your future starts now. Today won't wait forever.

How to Love Yourself 100%

Nothing is more important and more practical than having a healthy sense of self-worth, and this comes from loving yourself unreservedly. When the way you look at yourself is positive, then everything else about your life follows that path, and life becomes simpler, happier, and brighter.

Why is loving yourself important? Because every relationship you will have with someone else will reflect the relationship you have with yourself. If you love yourself wholeheartedly, you will love other people with the same fervor.

Far too many people look down on themselves or look to others for affirmation and validation. They feel low and needy, which results in one of two things: they either self-sabotage, or they start craving attention from other people.

Out of a lack of self-love can stem a greed for affection, looking to others for love. People with low self-esteem start doing things out of the wrong motivation and out of focus. They starve themselves to death just to be thin or sexy enough, work themselves to death just to be successful enough, expose themselves to exaggerated pain and suffering just to be accepted enough — and the list goes on. Lack of self-love is destructive.

It is true and right that we should love others. But you need to ask yourself if you are more interested in giving love to others than giving love to yourself. Loving yourself brings contentment, motivation, and focus — and that brings success and happiness.

You don't love yourself only when you are perfect. Nobody is perfect or will ever be perfect. But love looks beyond imperfections and brings out the best. So instead of beating yourself up and being hard on yourself, loving yourself 100% means that you accept all of who you are in your own flawed skin.

The best gift you can receive is YOURSELF — overflowing with self-love. This book is about practical ways to love yourself 100% so you can be the happiest and the best you can be. With patience, compassion, and willingness on your part to learn and adapt, this book will help you discover and build a foundation and understanding of what matters most: LOVING YOURSELF UNCONDITIONALLY.

Step Out Into the Limelight

"Remember always that you not only have the right to be an individual,
you have an obligation to be one."

- Eleanor Roosevelt

It's your time to shine.

The first step to loving yourself 100% is to know the true you. Focus on yourself and ask: *Who am I, really?*

You may find that it is difficult to give an answer to this simple question. Your initial responses may be based on how others have labeled you, what your occupation is, who your friends are, or which country you live in. But none of those things define you in the truest sense.

To have a sense of reality beyond external perceptions, you can start by making a list of the things that you feel make up the person you are right now, such as:

Character traits

Skills

Thoughts

Personal beliefs

Values

Dreams

To get an honest evaluation, be sure to list both virtues and vices that you have. It is good to recognize both positive and less desirable traits. While doing this, take time to appreciate and value yourself. List the things that make you unique and dwell on those. Remember that you are different from everyone else, and that is a good thing.

After you complete that list, make a decision to stop trying to blend in. Conformity is tantamount to a humdrum existence. It doesn't matter if you are different from everyone else or if people just don't get you. Bring out the real you, and do your own thing without restraint.

Think about what Dr. Seuss said and feel proud of yourself: "Today you are You, that is truer than true. There is no one alive who is Youer than You."

Take Care of Yourself Every Day

"To love oneself is the beginning of a life-long romance."

- Oscar Wilde

The world around you constantly demands your attention and action. Every time you respond and do something for somebody else, you give away a piece of yourself. And when you share a piece of yourself with someone else, you need to replace it. Otherwise you will end up empty, worn out, and stressed. That is why you need to take care of yourself every day — this way you will replenish yourself.

If you find yourself constantly scuttling around activities, responsibilities, and relationships, you will eventually be exhausted. You must recognize that you need to take some time for yourself. It doesn't have to be an extreme course of action. Simply waking up an hour earlier than everyone else at home to read, do some reflection or exercise, or drink coffee by the window can bring such a boost to your life. You fill yourself by focusing your attention and energy *on yourself every single day.*

While that first idea is quite common and effective, it may not work well for everyone. We are all made different from each other, and we have different needs and different self-love tanks. Healthy ideas like meditation, workouts, and eating comfort foods are not the only ways to undo stress.

Taking care of yourself is as personal as it gets. You need to understand that rest and relaxation means different things to different people, so you have to develop your *own* routine. It can be any of the following: reading, taking a nap, watching television, cooking, indulging in a hot bath, or engaging in a hobby. Whatever it is that fits your fancy, be sure to include it in your daily life.

Before you make that list, keep this in mind: you need to make choices that are not based on other people's expectations. For example, just because you are a stay-at-home mom, it doesn't mean that you have to make a lot of DIY stuff or know how to cook and bake. Do something that will make you happy. Do something that is in keeping with your personal goals and values. And remember, no one does it perfectly. Perfection is not the goal; loving yourself is.

Be true to yourself; do what you think is most valuable and authentic to who you really are, because when you act on it, even after an exhausting day, you will be refreshed in a rewarding and fulfilling way.

Find ways to take care of your whole being — spirit, soul, and body — so that you can enjoy life to the fullest.

It is not a Sin to Pamper Yourself

"A healthy self-love means we have no compulsion to justify ourselves or others why we take vacations, why we sleep late, why we buy new shoes, why we spoil ourselves from time to time. We feel comfortable doing things which add quality and beauty to life."

- Andrew Matthews

You only get one body, so be good to it and smother it with lavish love! Make an effort every day to pamper yourself. This means engaging in an activity that will make you feel good and happy. It can be a trip to the salon, a cup of coffee, or dancing to your favorite music. When you find something that will make you feel joyful, do it. Do it for yourself and not for anyone else.

Remember that *me time* is essential to self-love, happiness, and health.

Here are some simple ways to de-stress and recharge your mind and body:

Shop for new bags, shoes, or clothes.

Listen to your favorite tunes.

Treat yourself to a massage or a spa treatment.

Ride a bike in the countryside or around the city.

Dress up and take yourself out on a date — solo! You'll be surprised at how liberating it feels.

Bake a cake and eat it, too.

Go on a weekend getaway.

Get a makeover.

Call a friend you haven't spoken to in a long time.

Try aromatherapy.

Soak in a hot bath for more than an hour.

Have a slumber party or a manicure-pedicure/spa party with friends.

Eat chocolate. Lots!

Put on some comfortable clothes and read a good book.

Give restorative yoga a shot.

Eat ice cream without guilt.

Get a little more sleep than usual.

Indulge in a movie marathon with popcorn on the side.

Spend quality time with people you love.

Play with a pet cat or dog.

One thing that can keep you from pampering yourself is a to-do list. It may always seem like you do not have enough time to complete everything. While it may be true, it will be fun and easier to love yourself if you forget about your list for a while and do something else.

It does not mean that you will be irresponsible; you will just give yourself a break. Oftentimes, breakthroughs from boredom and the daily rut come from experiencing amazing adventures and activities that are out of your comfort zone. Get out of your routine and do something exciting for a change. You will find that you have renewed energy and enthusiasm to complete the things in your to-do list, simply because you dedicated an amount of time to make yourself feel good.

Never, ever berate yourself or feel guilty when you treat yourself to simple pleasures that make you feel divine.

Remind yourself: you need it. You deserve it. It is fuel to your body and soul.

Never feel guilty for treating yourself kindly.

Self-Love is Spiritual

"Self-care is never a selfish act — it is simply good stewardship of the only gift I have, the gift I was put on earth to offer others."

- Parker Palmer

The Bible does not say you should only love others and not yourself. God loves you and wants you to love yourself because you are special. When you realize that you are a gift to others, you learn to love and care for yourself more. You understand that you have only one life, and you have to make the most of every opportunity to make it wonderful, beautiful, and magical.

Self-care means "I love me," but it is in no way selfish. Eating right, exercising regularly, taking vitamins, and getting enough sleep and rest are all about improving and maintaining your physical health. Being a good steward of your temple means loving yourself.

But self-care is more than just being a good steward of your body. It also entails giving due attention to your mind and soul.

Let it go. Grudges, bitterness, regrets, past mistakes — whatever it is you are holding on to, release it. You can do it mentally or you can do it symbolically — write it down or record it in your voice mail then destroy the "evidence" afterward. Forgive others, and forgive yourself, too. That is the key to living freely.

Be brave. Live boldly and do not miss out on life. Go beyond your fears, anxieties, and even exhaustion. Consider your talents, remember your strengths, believe in yourself, and just go for it! Fortune smiles upon the brave.

Be inclusive. Invite friends into your home or go out and have conversations over coffee. Show your interest and appreciation by including people in your life. Do not live your life online. Many people hide behind the Internet because they fear rejection and shun real-life connections. Social media is just a small part of life! Unplug and go out into the real world with real people.

Shine your light. When you truly love yourself, it shows. And you can encourage other people to love themselves, too. Remember that whatever you give will beam back at you.

Remind yourself that you are a gift to others. Be the torch that shines brightly by being a living example of self-love.

The Pot of Gold is in Your Hands

"To establish true self-esteem, we must concentrate on our successes and forget about the failures and the negatives in our lives."

- Denis Waitley

Sometimes life gets messy and you find yourself down in the dumps. There are many situations that you do not have control over, such as how people love or don't love you. However, you can always control how you see things and act upon them.

The roads of life aren't always filled with rainbows, and getting that proverbial pot of gold is entirely up to you. A key to happiness is to love yourself unconditionally. That pot of gold can be yours even at the beginning of the journey.

Remember that you are loved and lovable. Even when people say bad things about you or act unkindly toward you, it does not discredit the fact that you are amazing and beautiful. Think kindly about yourself.

When you are feeling down or hurt, remember the compliments that other people have given you. And even if no one has paid you a compliment, speak good things about yourself — *to yourself!* That is a pot of gold right there — encouraging, uplifting words.

As you go along in life, you will change and grow. As you adjust and adapt, you will become a better person. Keep track of your progress and celebrate milestones, big and small. Do you smile more? Do you meet deadlines better? Note the ways in which you have developed or improved yourself and rejoice. If there are things you still need to work on, then be happy still because you are getting there one step at a time.

Do not dwell on failures, mishaps, and other negative things that have happened to you. Learn all the lessons you can and keep moving forward. While on the road, remember the times you have actually made it, and celebrate. Go out and have a drink or bake a cake in remembrance of your progress.

Each success you mark is a gold nugget added to your pot — bringing you more happiness and more love for yourself.

Always dwell on the positive things about yourself: list your achievements, acknowledge your progress, and celebrate your successes in life.

Find the Hidden Gifts

"Who looks outside, dreams; who looks inside, awakes."

- Carl Gustav Jung

Life is but a sum of days one after another, filled with details big and small. How you decide to spend each day will determine the quality of life that you lead. You can't simply live idly, letting life pass you by and just going about your mundane routine from sunup to sundown. You are not meant to merely survive. You need to live life with purpose. Some days may be great, while others may be so-so. Nevertheless, treat each day as an essential gift that holds many promises.

Making the right choices brings success in life. And you make the first right choice the moment you open your eyes in the morning. Decide that no matter what happens or doesn't happen, you will make the most of your day today and find the hidden gifts that life has for you. There are precious gems each day that you can unearth to make you love yourself a bit more. Be intentional about finding the hidden gifts that each day brings.

Breathe more life into your day by doing something that you love daily and focusing on your goals and dreams, your hopes and ambitions. You will be amazed to find that opportunities and open doors are right before you, and you can step into them, toward success.

Schedule enough rest, and do not feel guilty when you do. Always look inside of yourself. Know what you need and attend to that need. Awaken to more possibilities and be more effective.

Be completely present when you are with others. In this day and age where technology has taken up a great part of life, you need to learn to engage fully. When you give your consideration to others and to what is happening around you, you will find that you are rewarding yourself in the process. Put away stuff that may distract you from interpersonal connections. Pay attention to the small things the same way you notice the big things. Remember that relationships enrich life.

Sometimes doing what you want requires sacrifices. Spending time and effort on a hobby may mean time away from family. Learning a new skill may require hours of classes and tests. Going on a trip abroad may cost a huge amount of money. But sacrifices will always be worth it, especially if you do things because you love yourself.

Do not be afraid to surrender to be happier. Think about this: a seed dies as soon as it is planted into the ground, but then new life springs out of it. And that new life brings out something bigger than what the seed started out from. A mango seed becomes a mango tree, and from one come hundreds more.

Keep in mind that harvest comes only when something is planted. Think of sacrifice as a seed. When you sow or give up something, you will always reap something more.

Express yourself daily. Draw, sing, blog, sew, write a letter, tweet — anything that will express who you are. Be creative and take pleasure in what lights up your life. Dress up and put makeup on, even if you are just staying home for the day. Get out in the sun. Not only will the vitamin D be good for your skin and bones, but getting out there will induce happy hormones, which will make you feel lighter and jollier.

Express love every single day — to yourself and to other people. Give a hug, a kiss, a simple smile, or a pat on the shoulder. And those three little words, "I love you?" Don't be afraid to say them. Be unconditional in expressing your love.

If you are going through a storm in life, do not fret. Always look for that silver lining and trust that morning always comes after the night. Perseverance will take you places. It is the time to love yourself more and focus on what will make you strong. And you will be more resilient and fearless after you go through a tough time, ready to face greater things ahead.

When you find yourself in a rut or a bad situation at the end of one day, don't stay stuck in it. Loving yourself means you wake up the next day and decide to do better. You choose to do what is right and continue to look forward to gifts and blessings that the new day brings.

Make the most of every day. Notice the little things that make life beautiful and value them.

Guard Your Heart With All Diligence

"Guard your heart with all diligence, for out of it springs the issues of life."

- King Solomon

Your heart is the central element of who you really are, the essence of your being. The heart is the wellspring of life. Make it your priority to guard your heart. Always remember that everything comes from the heart. It is like a fountain where your thoughts overflow and become words and deeds. It is a source that should not be plugged up or poisoned. It will impact everything about your life: your family, your friends, your career, your present, and your future.

Do not let your heart take in garbage. Here's a rule: no garbage in, all garbage out. Fill your heart with words and thoughts that are kind, true, noble, pure, and trustworthy. If situations and relationships throw rubbish your way, you have the right refuse to let it into your heart.

Do not stress your heart by dwelling on the past. Today is a gift. Live in it. When you find yourself holding on to things that have hurt you or disappointments over what could have been, stop. Give yourself room and the chance to experience new joys — new plans, people, places, and things to come your way. Focus on what is productive and meaningful.

Set aside time to be still and meditate. Be receptive to love, affection, and attention from God and those around you. Deliberately think about the amazing things that make you happy — things that are a source of pleasure and inspiration. This will help you maintain an open heart. A natural response that most people take when they are hurt or facing tough times is to protect their hearts from the pain. Rightly so, but you need to open up your heart again and let it grow and change. It will be easy to love yourself this way as sincerity finds its way to your heart. It will bring about an outward expression of love as well.

Guarding your heart is not simple, but you need to be courageous and work hard to do this. Consider Charles Dickens' famous words: "Have a heart that never hardens, and a temper that never tires, and a touch that never hurts." Your life will be defined by what comes from your heart. So have a good heart — strong yet soft.

Your world will only be as big as your heart. Shield your heart from pain, but never close it from love.

Self-Respect is Real Power

"No one can make you feel inferior without your consent."

- Eleanor Roosevelt

Loving yourself entails self-respect. It will develop your potential and let everyone realize that you are someone who is worthy of respect. Accept yourself and make every effort to become the better person you have always wanted to be. Be happy with who you are and make the world respect you as you deserve.

You need to embrace yourself with all your flaws and be happy with who you are and what you have. Stop making excuses for what you are not and what you don't have.

Believe in your decisions and trust your judgment. You have to be firm in your beliefs and make an effort to appreciate yourself and to know what will really make you happy.

From time to time, reward yourself for a decision well made. Valuing yourself means that once you have made a decision, you stick to that choice no matter how difficult it may be.

Here are some important pieces of advice you can follow in order to help you respect yourself more:

Discern when people disrespect you and take the necessary action to put a stop to it. Do not allow others to treat you badly. Learn to let disrespectful people go, even if it is hard.

Never allow people to trample on you and make you feel terrible. Cut off all connections with such people. It will be difficult for you to build self-respect if you continually associate with people who cannot offer you basic respect.

When there is a need for you to confront others about their disrespectful behavior, be sure to communicate positively.

There is no reason to be mean when other people are. Be the bigger person.

Learn to take criticism. If people say something helpful, then listen and make room for self-improvement. Constructive criticism builds you up and allows you to reach your goals. If someone is being hurtful, then throw whatever was said out of the window. Do not allow people's words to hurt you or scar you for life. Learn to discern what is constructive and what is just plain cruel, as you see yourself as someone who can be better.

You need to know when someone is being manipulative or controlling. Do not let people use you. Stop being needy and stop being a people pleaser; you do not need to depend on anyone for happiness.

Famous actor and Academy Award-winning director and producer Clint Eastwood once said, "Respect your efforts, respect yourself. Self-respect leads to self-discipline. When you have both firmly under your belt, that's real power." Have that real power in your life as you love yourself 100%.

Respect yourself completely and don't accept anything less from anyone else.

Dare to Dream Again

"It is never too late to be what you might have been."

- George Eliot

Seize the moment. Today is the day to try out something new, become a better person, or to get on that adventure you have always dreamed of. It is never too late to do what you really desire to do. It may be a childhood dream, teenage aspirations, or even a professional ambition. You just need to go for it.

If you have allowed other people's opinions to hold you back and their criticisms to stop you and instill fear in you, then throw caution to the wind. If certain past experiences prevent you from venturing out again, believe in second, third, and many more chances! Do not live in regret. Dare to dream, and dream big!

Do something that you have never done before, something you have never even thought of before. Innovate. Create. In the process, you will discover new strengths, new skills, and new self-respect.

You need to set goals — enormous goals. Set goals that are lofty, goals that almost seem impossible to achieve. Do not settle for average. Do not settle for something that can be easily achieved. You deserve better than mediocrity. Remind yourself that you deserve the best. When you work toward these goals, you will see yourself in a better light. When you achieve these goals, you will love yourself more.

Do not rest on your achievements. Tell yourself that it can be boring when you're already on top of something. When you do something you are good at over and over again, it is just mundane. Challenge yourself every day to be better than your best, to go beyond the laurels you have made for yourself.

Do something you have been afraid to do. Shake up your routine and gather up the courage to do a big thing. Maybe you want to learn how to bake; enroll yourself in a class. Maybe you want to set up a business. Then do so, by all means. Would you like to go to another country and experience another culture? Go cliff diving, bungee jumping, zip lining, or do other extreme activities? Write a book? Record an album? There are no limits to your dreams. You can do it if you set your mind, heart, and soul on it. Be a superhero — for yourself. Make your life beautiful and exciting in big and small ways. Rescue yourself from the dull and dreary.

When you dream, remind yourself to carry on with your own agenda in mind. Do not mold your dreams according to what other people expect or demand of you. Hang on to who you are and what you dream of — not the world's standards. When you do this, remind yourself that it is you — not things or the people around you — that make yourself happy.

Steer clear of people who try to put down your faith in your goals and ambitions. You need to push past them and follow your dreams. Keep moving forward all the time.

When you dare to dream, you love yourself. Charting a course and following your dreams will connect you to yourself more. This will bring a defining strength to your life and a sense of magic to your days. You dream because you have a choice, and when that fact is settled in your heart, you can overcome any failure or fear that you will face in the pursuit of your dream.

Make magic every day by dreaming and reaching for the stars.

Be Thankful Every Day

"I will praise Thee; for I am fearfully and wonderfully made: marvelous are Thy works; and that my soul knoweth very well."

- Psalms 139:14, King James Bible

A lot of people consider themselves ugly, stupid, dumb, worthless, and all the other negative things one can imagine. If you realize that you are created in the image and likeness of God, then your thinking will change.

Instead of looking at the mirror and saying "I am ugly" or "No one cares about me," look at yourself and say, "I am wonderful. I am beautiful. I am smart. I am strong. I can take on the world!" God did not fail when He created you, and you are certainly wonderfully made for success. Know this in your heart, and you will learn to love yourself more. This will result in your appreciation of the things and people around you.

It is sad when you hear people grumble, "Woe is me. I don't like my job," when there are a million other people who are unemployed or are seriously overworked and underpaid, or when you hear people say ridiculous complaints like, "The beach isn't sandy enough," or "The air-conditioning isn't cool enough." Whatever you are going through in life, there will always, *always* be something to be thankful about.

Make a list of the things that you can be thankful for every day. Here are some examples:

For good health, which means more than any amount of money

For the house you live in (no matter the size)

For the job that puts food on the table

For parents who brought you into the world

For children who bring happiness (even though they can sometimes cause such a mess!)

For phones and the Internet that allow you to communicate with other people, near or far

For laundry, because it means you have clothes to wear

For dishes in the sink, because it means you had food to eat

For friends who stick by you through thick and thin

For people who don't like you, because that means you are a unique individual with a different set of values

For that extra hour of sleep

For strangers who have gone out of their way to help you or make you smile

For water, being a very precious necessity that not everyone has access to

For music, which brings beauty to the soul

For failures, suffering, and pain that teach you to become stronger

For the ability to help others in need

For hugs and kisses and other acts of love that are given to you and that you can give back

For waking up today and getting another chance in life

It is important to be thankful for things that make you happy, things that keep you comfortable, things that sustain your every need, and things that help you change and become a better person. Whether your days are exciting or annoying, remain thankful. Even if bad things happen, how you respond will define your life: forlorn and immobilized or thankful and rising up.

Another key to having a thankful heart is to never compare yourself or your situation to others. Be grateful for what you have, because if you focus on what you *don't* have, then you will never have enough! An attitude of gratitude will help you overcome worry, self-doubt, helplessness, frustration, and fear. Thankfulness gives you the power to move in a positive direction every single day.

Gratitude makes you love yourself completely, as you see and appreciate all the things that make your life beautiful. You attract to your life those that you recognize and appreciate.

Wake up every morning with a grateful heart. There is always something to be thankful for every day.

Reach Out in Love

"The purpose of life is not to be happy. It is to be useful, to be honorable, to be compassionate, to have it make some difference that you have lived and lived well."

- Ralph Waldo Emerson

To love yourself completely will equate to loving other people as well. Reach out and touch a life today. This will make you live out of an overflow of love in your life, which will return to you in the form of love as well.

How can you love people and be a beam of sunshine in their lives?

Live with integrity. Be honest and kind. Mean what you say and say what you mean. Do not be mean, and use your words to encourage and uplift people. Do the right thing even when no one is watching.

Respect people regardless of their status in life. Everyone deserves respect. When you give people esteem that is due them, you can be sure to get it back.

Stop judging. Do your very best to refrain from criticizing others — the way they act, what they wear, how they speak. Do you know that what you don't use, you will eventually lose? Silence that nitpicking voice inside you, and you will become a happier person.

Reach out to others regularly. Do something to connect with other people. You can start by talking about yourself, what you are going through, how you feel, what you need — this will help you stay in touch. You can go from there and listen to other people's interests and concerns. Reaching out will help you avoid being sad or depressed and can be a channel of inspiration to you and others.

Be compassionate and do your best to understand people, especially those who are totally different from you.

Pursue peace with everyone.

Do not stay mad for a long time.

Smile.

Make people feel good about themselves. Express your love and appreciation every way you can. When you do that, you will feel good about yourself, too. The more love you give out, the more it builds inside of you.

Volunteer for community work. Choose something that is relevant to your values and make an effort to help. You can give your time, money, or influence for a good cause.

How you reach out in love will characterize your life, and if you give it your best effort, it will be revolutionary!

Define your life by the way you reach out to others in love and compassion. Honor others, be helpful, be constructive, and make others happy.

Recognize that you are a miracle and you can make a difference in someone else's life.

How to Apply What You've Learned

Let these thoughts transform your life by putting them to action. Make a decision every day to love yourself completely by following the simple ideas outlined in this book. The change won't happen in a day, so be sure to set realistic expectations. The process won't be seamless, but the rewards will be most gratifying. Your aim is not to be perfect, but to love yourself 100%.

Think about what Dr. Seuss said and feel proud of yourself: "Today you are You, that is truer than true. There is no one alive who is Youer than You."

Remind yourself today and every day that YOU are unique. You do not have to be perfect in order to be special. You do not have to be like everybody else. You have a responsibility to be your true self.

Find ways to take care of your whole being — spirit, soul, and body — so that you can enjoy life to the fullest.

Make sure that you are not left empty. Take time to fill yourself up through various activities that will refresh your body, soul, and spirit. Enjoy life by giving to others and giving to yourself as well.

Never feel guilty for treating yourself kindly.

Remember that it is never wrong to pamper yourself and to regard yourself highly.

Remind yourself that you are a gift to others. Be the torch that shines brightly by being a living example of self-love.

Loving yourself is sacred. When you love yourself, it oozes out of you, and people are positively affected. Constantly prompt yourself that you are a gift to people and utilize that as an encouragement to love yourself more.

Always dwell on the positive things about you: list your achievements, acknowledge your progress, and celebrate your successes in life.

Never rest on your laurels, and do not allow yourself to be held back by fear or failure. Remind yourself of the times you have succeeded or felt good about something. When you fail or when someone finds fault in you, remind yourself of the pleasant stuff about you and move on. Always look at the bright side of life.

Make the most of every day: Notice the little things that make life beautiful.

Life is filled with many beautiful things, so take time to find those hidden beautiful things. Search out and appreciate that smile from a child, the bloom in your garden, the wind on your face, the opportunity to be kind to someone else. Love yourself more by valuing what every day brings your way.

Your world will only be as big as your heart. Shield your heart from pain, but never close it from love.

Make every effort to guard your heart diligently. Never allow rubbish in by always filling your heart with love. Let your life be an overflow of love.

Respect yourself completely, and don't accept anything less from anyone else.

Never allow other people to treat you unkindly. Sometimes when you want people to accept you, you allow them to use and manipulate you, and you lose your self-respect. Always guard your heart and be quick to cut off wrong associations.

Make magic every day by dreaming and reaching for the stars.

Aspire for more for your life. No dream is too far-fetched, and no desire is too insignificant for your life. Being a dreamer won't mean your head will always be in the clouds.

It just means that you love yourself enough to go beyond where you are now. Don't let people talk you out of pursuing your dreams.

Wake up every morning with a grateful heart. There is always something to be thankful for every day.

Cultivate an attitude of gratitude, and recognize the value of things and people that are in your life. Thankfulness makes your life more meaningful. Be thankful for who you are and what you have.

Recognize that you are a miracle and you can make a difference in someone else's life.

You are the best thing that has ever happened to you — and the world. The world is a better place because you are in it. You, with all that you are, strengths and talents, weaknesses and shortcomings, are a miracle for someone. Always put this fact in your heart and mind, and you will appreciate and love yourself more. Make your mark in someone's life and expect it to come back to you. Do something to make their life happier, and you will find yourself happier, too.

As you pursue the practice of absolutely loving yourself, never let anyone's expectation dampen your spirits or keep you from your goal. Love yourself today, more than the previous day. Self-love is not a sin, and you can only love others with the love that you have for yourself.

Take one day at a time to do the things that will help you love yourself unconditionally, and you will soon find yourself in that place where you love the most important person of all — YOU!

How To Open Your Spiritual Chakras

You are probably wondering why you need to learn about chakras and how to open them. In a world of uncertainties and chaos, it is easy for one to get lost, add to how fast pace a lot of people's lives are. It is easy to succumb to unhealthy eating, negative thoughts, and overall unbeneficial health habits, resulting to an imbalance life. But health deterioration - physically, mentally, and spiritually - should not be taken for granted.

People need to bring back that balance of energy back to feel healthy once again.

In a nutshell, chakras are the main energy centers within your body. They actually exist because you can feel them! They can affect and are also affected by every thought, every sense, every feeling, and every experience that you have. For instance, when you feel strongly about something, you know it's your "gut feel" - that is actually one of the seven chakras.

This book will help you open up your chakras to restore the balance of energy in your body. Tuning into these energies will help integrate your consciousness so you become mindful and see more clearly, thus making it easier to analyze and solve problems or challenges that come your way.

Opening up your chakras will also help you find that inner peace, so you become more mindful and enjoy your life the way you should.

From this book, you will learn the basics of the spiritual chakras, how to increase energy, and some useful techniques that you can use to open up your chakras.

Take on that journey towards the path of enlightenment through this book.

What are Spiritual Chakras?

"As we explore the aura and the chakras, it is important for us to view our journey not as revolutionary, but rather as very traditional. Chakras, as well as auras and electromagnetic fields are as old as the earth itself. The chakra system, in fact, is a part of the ancient and lost mysteries. And, in the end, the chakra system in our bodies is how we find our way back to the most ancient mystery of all – God, the Oneness, the Omniscient."

- Rosalyn L. Bruyere, Wheels of Light

Spiritual energy has been known and used by ancient traditions. This is evident in Chinese medicine which built their health care around the principles of acupuncture. Most of the popular native traditions are focused around the use of natural energies of the human body for healing.

Common to all these traditions is the premise that energy has centers or focal points of congregation at different places in the body. These energy centers are called by many different names, but the most common term used is "chakras".

What is a Chakra?

Chakra is a Sanskrit term meaning "vortex of energy". The number of energy centers is different from tradition to tradition. With Chinese medicine, there are more than a hundred acupuncture points; on the other hand, most martial arts traditions only have one energy point, called the hara. Still, there are others that have 5 to 10.

The most common traditions have 7 energy centers and these primary energies will be the point of discussion in this book.

The 7 chakras are vertically aligned along the stretch of your back, starting from the top of your head up to below the bottom of your spine. Each one of these chakras is equivalent to a wave field without the particles, just pure potential. When these energy points are opened, their appearance is similar to the other side of the Black Hole where the energy streams out as opposed to coming in.

The frequency and quality of energy from each chakra differ because each of them is considered to have its own type of spiritual energy or its own tuning. The energy points can initially be found and identified as void spaces or pure energy fields. The spiritual energy is considered immeasurable, the term used in Chinese medicine as the "chi". Power can flow through the chakras only if they are activated or opened.

On a technical standpoint, the chakras are the fields wherein energies flow, and not necessarily the spiritual energies themselves. A chakra can be likened to a door which needs to be opened.

*Key Points/Action Steps

The primary point of this chapter is that the chakras are energy centers that help us attain a healthy state. The best thing to do now is to learn more about them in the succeeding chapters. Understand the next chapter for it will give you more information about the Seven Chakra System.

The Seven Chakras System

"Chakras are energy-awareness centers. They are the revolving doors of creativity and communication between spirit and the world."

- Michael J. Tamura

The literal translation of *chakra* is *wheel*. Each of the seven chakras has specific qualities which correspond to the refinement of energy from the base level of your material-self-identity. These energy centers are representations of the highest level of integration split similar to a prism, into a spectrum of different colors.

The chakras are shaped where the three energy shafts meet; ascending the spine, there is one on each side of the central channel, called the *Shushumna*. The *Pingala* (on the right) and the *Ida* (on the left) are the lesser channels of energy, they are parallel to your spinal cord. Your chakras take up and collect the *prana* or life force energy. They also transform and pass on energy. Your "material body" cannot exist without these energy points because they are the gateways through which energy flows, giving life to your physical body.

Each of the 7 chakra is associated with a particular part of the body and a specific organ to provide energy from. Similar to how each of your organs has its equivalent on your spiritual and mental levels; each chakra has a corresponding human behavior and development linked to it.

The circular spirals have different sizes and perform a variety of activities because no two people are alike. They also vibrate at varying levels which can be linked to your own individual awareness and the chakras' ability to integrate into your life. For instance, the lower chakras are related to your fundamental emotions and needs, since they vibrate at a lower frequency, thus denser. The finer energies of the upper chakras are linked to the higher spiritual and mental aspirations and faculties.

The energy flow and openness through your own chakras determine the balance of energies in your body and your state of health. When you become more aware of your more subtle energy system, you are empowered to maintain the balance and harmony of your mental, spiritual, and physical levels.

Yoga masters and meditation experts aim to balance out the energy of your chakras by effectively purifying your lower energies and guiding them all the way up. With the use of different tools and methods, like grounding, or creating internal space, or living consciously with certain awareness on how your body needs to get and spend energy in order to achieve a sense of balance in all aspects of your life.

*Key Points/Action Steps

The 7 chakras are strategically positioned in your body, in order to open them up; you have to be aware where they are located. Study where they are each located so it will be easier for you to apply the techniques that you will learn in the succeeding chapters.

Crown Chakra
Sahasrara

"Never be afraid to sit awhile and think."

- Lorraine Hansberry, A Raisin in the Sun

The *Crown Chakra* is considered to be the 7th Chakra.

Location: Top of the Head

Color Representation: Violet

Symbol: The Lotus with a Thousand Petals

Corresponding Organ/Body Parts: Pineal Gland

Spinal Pair: Root Chakra (7/1)

Gem: Pearl

Planet: Pluto

Overflowing: Ego maniac, cult leader

Lacking: No spiritual aspiration

Element: Spirit

The Shiva or Consciousness

This 7th Chakra is considered to be the content-free field of your imagination that has the capability to receive "renewing light". It makes you aware that you are a part of the whole universe.

This chakra is the representation of the highest level of consciousness and enlightenment. It is your connection to the center of the spirit. This is where all the other chakras are integrated together with their own unique qualities. Your ability to master the lower vibrational aspect of your whole being allows you to become fully aware that you are in fact a spiritual being who lives a "human" existence.

It is your link to divine oneness. It is the source of inspiration and guidance.

How to Open the Crown Chakra

Meditation is known to be the best exercise to open up the *Crown Chakra*. There are different forms of meditation and you can apply most of them when you want to open your 7th Chakra.

You can perform the traditional meditation techniques wherein you simply sit comfortably and meditate until you reach a state of calmness, peace, and oneness with nature. You can utter a daily mantra or create images in your head to help you free your mind from worries, doubts, and problems, so you can go to the "plane" of peace and serenity.

It is important, however, that you have to know your biggest challenge in becoming successful in mediation, and this is your attachments on material and earthly things. Material possessions and negative ideas prevent you from successfully opening up your *Crown Chakra*.

When you really want to achieve that certain level of calmness, you have to be open to aggressively "using" and manifesting your *Crown Chakra*.

For instance, instead of saying, *"I will eat this specific dish for dinner"*, you can use these words, *"I would like to eat something that will make me feel happy and wonderful"*. This technique opens you up to new and better ideas and thoughts which can help you in opening up your chakra. Emptying your mind completely takes practice. Opening up your *Crown Chakra* is not just about lifting your energy up, but it also involves moving it down so that your desires manifest.

The Crystals

The *Crown Chakra* can be represented by purple or white. To help in opening up your chakra, there are crystals that you can use that have specific purposes:

Celestite – Balancing, Aligning, Opening

244

Clear Topaz – Activating

Amethyst – Balancing and Clearing

Danburite – Opening, Clearing, Stimulating

Phenacite – Activating and Opening

Optical Calcite – Stimulating

Clear Quartz – Activating, Balancing, Clearing, Aligning

Rutilated Quartz – Activating, Balancing, Clearing

Selenite – Balancing

*Key Points/Action Steps

The *Crown Chakra* is the center of your consciousness. What you do in life starts from your thoughts, when this chakra is properly opened and utilized, you easily attain a certain level of being one with the universe. When you successfully empty your mind with unnecessary thoughts, you achieve a level of peace and calmness and your desires are manifested.

Learn meditation techniques because this will help you reach the needed level of peace, harmony, and calmness.

Third Eye Chakra
Ajna

"We have five senses in which we glory and which we recognize and celebrate, sense that constitute the sensible world for us. But here are other senses – secret senses, sixth senses, if you will – equally vital, but unrecognized, and unlauded."

-Oliver Sacks

The *Third Eye Chakra* is the 6th Chakra.

Location*:* Forehead

Color Representation*:* Indigo

Symbol*:* Descending Triangle within a Circle

Seed Mantra*:* Aum

Corresponding Organ/Body Parts: Pituitary gland, lower brain, spine, nose, left eye, both ears

Spinal Pair*:* Sacral Chakra (6/2)

Gem: Diamond

Planet: Sun

Sense: Higher mind, sixth sense

Overflowing: Overly analytical/intellectual

Lacking: Deluded

Element: Light

Knowingness / Intuition / Perception

It is in this 6th Chakra that you visualize things through your *third eye*. It is considered to be the seat of intuition and spiritual vision. When you open up your *third eye,* you experience a spiritual awakening. This is also known as the chakra of compassion and forgiveness.

How to Open the Third Eye Chakra

The 6th Chakra is associated with the light and imagination; you will use these two in opening up this chakra. You need to "capture" the light each time you experience it and bring it inside you. Here's a simple technique:

The next time you see a beautiful sunset, open up your entire awareness and imagine yourself absorbing the light.

Close your eyes and create a mental image of the sunset using your third eye. Continue doing this exercise until you can easily "summon" the image at will.

This exercise can be done even without an amazing sunset because you can apply its principles when you experience and see a colorful display of light. Take advantage of the light that you see coming off your car's windshield, or observe how sunlight makes on trees during the blowing of the wind, or observe how the light coming from a candle makes a play on the lighted area during one of your meditation sessions. As long as there is a play of colors and light, you can perform this technique.

The Crystals

Each one of us is connected to everyone and to everything. When this chakra is blocked, you fail to recognize the patterns that you see all around you, plus, you fail to hear your own intuition. These crystals will help you open up your third eye and create a balance of all your energies:

Amethyst – Opening, Stimulating, Balancing

Moldavite – Activating, Opening, Clearing

Herkimer Diamond – Activating

Indigo Aura – Stimulating

Howlite – Activating and Opening

Lolite – Opening and Clearing

Pietersite – Activating

Ruby Zoisite – Opening

Labradorite – Regulating

Stilbite – Stimulating

Azurite – Opening

Unakite – Grounding, Balancing, Aligning

When you meditate using any of these crystals, you have to focus on oneness. Know that we all come from one single source and we have to "wake up" to realize who we truly are. When you open up this chakra, you will be able to understand and maintain an open mind so you can hear the truth.

Key Points/Action Steps

The 6th Chakra makes you aware of your inner gut feel. When it is open, it is easier for you to make difficult decisions. Your intuition will guide you into which way you have to go. When you practice the "light and color" awareness exercise, you help open up your chakra. Constant practice is what you need to perfect this technique, so make sure that you do it each time you have the chance to experience beautiful colors or a play of light.

Throat Chakra
Vishuddha

"To speak and to speak well are two things. A fool may talk, but a wise man speaks."

– Ben Johnson

This is the 5th Chakra.

Location*:* Throat

Color Representation*:* Light Blue

Symbol*:* A circle within a descending triangle

Seed Mantra*:* Hum

Corresponding Organ/Body Parts: Throat, thyroid gland, upper lungs, digestive track, arms

Spinal Pair*:* Solar Chakra (5/3)

Gem*:* Sapphire

Planet: Saturn

Sense: Hearing

Overflowing: Controlling, will-full, hurtful speech, judgmental

Lacking: Cannot creatively express, lacking in faith

Element: Ether

Communication / Self-Expression / Sound / Creativity / Intuition / Desire to Speak and Hear the Truth

The 5th Chakra is the center for communication, creativity, and self-expression. This is where you find the inner voice of one's truth is fully expressed. This is the chakra of pure relationships with others, playful detachment, and diplomacy.

How to Open the Throat Chakra

The *Throat Chakra* works with vibrations and sounds. A powerful meditation with the use of the seed sounds of the chakras helps you open this up. The seed sounds were given in the ancient texts, also known as *bija mantras*. All you can do is repeat the sounds over and over at a certain rhythm that is comfortable for you. You go slowly when you want to calm the chakras, and go fast when you want them stimulated. It is even more effective if you sing the mantras in a single tone. Experiment on what will work well with you. The chakra sounds are: 1. Lam, 2. Vam, 3. Ram, 4. Yam, 5. Ham, 6. Ksham, and 7. Silence.

Use Crystals

In order to "heal" the *Throat Chakra,* you have to be honest to yourself and to the people around you.

The crystals that are associated with this chakra are the following:

Aqua Aura – Balancing and Activating

Apatite – Activating and Opening

Blue Lace Agate – Balancing

Turquoise – Balancing and Stimulating

Blue Tiger Eye – Soothing

Aquamarine – Activating and Clearing

Blue Calcite – Clearing

Blue Kyanite – Opening

Angelite – Clearing and Healing

Lapis Lazuli – Balancing, Activating, Opening

Sodalite – Stimulating

When meditating to open this chakra, better ask yourself if you have said things that might have hurt the feelings of other people. You also have to ask yourself how well you are expressing the things you need to express. Most of the time, the imbalance in the *Throat Chakra* is linked to physical sickness, like sore throat, so you have to take care of your health as well.

Key Points/Action Steps

This chakra is the center of communication, self-expression, and the desire to speak and hear the truth. It is important because you cannot deal with people if you don't know how to communicate with them. You cannot form relationships without proper self-expression. Honesty is an integral part in any relationships. In making sure that this chakra is open, you form honest and true relationships.

Learn the secrets of meditating and using the different sounds to open this chakra. Take care of your health, especially your throat since any illness affects your chakra's "health".

Heart Chakra
Anahata

"The first and highest law must be the love of a man to man. Homo homini Deus est – this is the supreme practical maxim, this is the turning point of the world's History.

– Ludwig Feuerbach, The Essence of Christianity

This is the 4th Chakra, "The Un-struck"

Location*:* Center of the chest

Color Representation*:* Green or Pink

Symbol*:* Interwined descending and ascending triangles

Seed Mantra*:* Yum

Corresponding Organ/Body Parts*:* Heart, thymus, blood circulation, lungs, liver

Spinal Pair*:* The Center (4/4)

Gem: Ruby

Planet: Venus

Sense: Touch

Overflowing: Poor emotional boundaries, inappropriate emotional expression

Lacking: Heartless, ruthless, can't feel any emotions

Element: Air

Love / Compassion / Desire for Self-Acceptance / Open-Hearted

The 4th Chakra is the center of true and unconditional expression of affection, compassion, love, devotion, and spiritual growth. It is considered to be the bridge that connects the lower and the higher energies. It is also the place where the Spirit and your True Self resides.

How to Open the 4th Chakra

The 4th Chakra relates to the element of air, thus, to open this up, you will need to work with your breath.

This technique will help expand your heart:

Sit in a comfortable posture, with an erect spine and eyes closed, as you get in tune with your heart. Begin with a slow rhythm of inhaling and exhaling. Imagine inhaling on your left side (receptive), and feel your heart expand. Take a few breaths, and then imagine your heart expanding on the right side (expressive), feel the space on your heart widen. Next, breathe into the bottom of your heart, this helps deepen your compassion for others and for yourself. After another few breaths, imagine breathing into the top part of your heart, lifting the heart to expand into your shoulders. Lastly, inhale while pushing your heart energy forward, as if you are putting it out into the world.

Use Crystals

Aside from love, the *Heart Chakra* is also linked to grief. When you are able to open up this chakra, you become more compassionate and loving. It also helps you deal easily with grief.

The crystals that you can use to help you open up this chakra are:

Jade – Balancing

Green Aventurine – Healing

Rose Quartz – Opening and Healing

Emerald – Opening

Lithium Quartz – Activating, Healing, Balancing

Ruby – Activating and Opening

Chrome Diopside – Opening and Healing

Peridot – Awakening

Green Tourmaline – Activating and Opening

Green Kyanite – Connecting the Third Eye to the Heart

*Key Points/Action Steps

This is the center because our whole being depends on it: true and unconditional feelings of love. Opening this up helps us to show compassion and love, not just to ourselves, but to humankind as a whole.

Meditating and breathing techniques are what you need to successfully open this chakra. Dutifully practice the techniques you learned above and use any of the crystals so you can open up your *Heart Chakra* in no time.

Solar Plexus Chakra
Manipura

"He who knows others is learned; he who knows himself is wise."

– Lao Tzu, Tao te Ching

This is 3rd Chakra.

Location: Slightly above the naval area

Color Representation: Yellow

Symbol: A descending triangle

Seed Mantra: Ram

Corresponding Organ/Body Parts: Stomach, pancreas, gallbladder, liver

Spinal Pair: Throat Chakra (3/5)

Sense: Sight

Gem: Emerald

Planet: Jupiter

Overflowing: Self-absorbed, egotistical, ambitious, desire to always take control

Lacking: Poor self-worth, martyr, sensitive, needing to "do" everything at the same time

Element: Fire

Will Power / Motivation / Joy

The 3rd Chakra is located at the center of your body, making it a place where your physical energy is distributed. This area is the center of unrefined emotions and personal power. This is the chakra that gives you a sense of contentment and ultimate satisfaction. Your will power fuels your creativity.

How to Open the Solar Plexus Chakra

For the 3rd Chakra, you will have to focus on developing your core strength because this will help increase power. Modified sit-ups, like stomach crunches, help build abdominal strength.

However, experts recommend the plank pose:

Lay on the floor, with your face down. Position your hands below the shoulders, keeping your arms straight. Lift your entire body off the ground, your toes curled under, and your body and legs forming a straight line, parallel to the floor. Hold this position for a minute. Challenge yourself by balancing on your forearms, with your elbows directly under your shoulders or alternately life each leg off the floor and hold that position.

Use Crystals

This chakra is associated with ego and pride. When you are able to open the *Solar Plexus Chakra,* you become aware of your deepest motivations in doing the things you do. It also boosts your confidence and empowers you to do what you need to do.

The crystals that you can use are:

Citrine – Cleansing

Topaz – Healing

Sunstone – Activating

Tiger's Eye – Healing and Balance

Amber – Energizing and Protecting

*Key Points/Action Steps

When this chakra is not "healed", you experience false pride and your ego jumps to the roof. This chakra is also the source of your strength and will power. When you open it up, you discover what drives you to do the things you, and at the same time, gives you the push to do what you have to do. It works two ways, to give you strength and confidence, but also nurtures your pride and ego when there is an imbalance.

You can work on the imbalance by doing the exercise technique given here. It takes a lot of practice, especially if you are not a physical person but with determination, you will be able to perfect it. You may also take advantage of the crystals provided here for you.

Sacral Chakra
Swadhishtana

"Do what makes you happy, be with who makes you smile, laugh as much as you breathe, and loves as long as you live."

– Rachel Ann Nunes

This is the 2nd Chakra.

Location: Slightly below the naval area

Color Representation: Orange

Symbol: An up-turned crescent

Seed Mantra: Vam

Corresponding Organ/Body Parts: Legs, reproductive organs, gonads

Spinal Pair: Third Eye (2/6)

Sense: Taste

Gem: Amethyst

Planet: Mercury

Overflowing: Lustful, controlling, addictive, and manipulative

Lacking: Submissive, co-dependent, martyr

Element: Water

Sexuality / Relationships / Pleasure / Empathy

The 2nd energy is the focal point of all of your relationships. This is where inner sense of self and the awareness of other people, your sexuality, ego, and your family are defined. When you are able to open up this chakra, it makes it easier for you to directly perceive what other people feel.

How to Open the Sacral Chakra

Since the 2nd Chakra has water as its element, it follows that the main purpose of this chakra is fluidity.

Do this exercise:

Find a crossed-legs Indian position style that is comfortable for you. Push the tip of your spine backward, while opening up your sacrum area, as you continuously expand and fill your lower belly. Imagine stretching your hips wide as you perform do this. Exhale, while moving your sacrum to the opposite direction, as you press on your navel towards your spine. Repeat the movements as you continue to let the energy flow all the way up to your spine.

Use Crystals

The 2nd Chakra is associated with relationships, blame, and guilt. If you want to "fix" this chakra, you have to learn to be honest, real, and open in all your relationships.

Use these crystals to help you open up this chakra:

Coral Calcite – Amplifier

Orange Carnelian – Healing

Orange Calcite – Activating and Cleansing

Snowflake Obsidian – Calming

Orange Aventurine – Opening

Moonstone – Balancing

Leopardskin Jasper – Protecting

*Key Points/Action Steps

This is the chakra related to all your relationships, your sexuality, sense of self, and your awareness of the people around you. If it is not properly opened, you tend to become unreasonably submission or the opposite, you become totally controlling. In order to open this chakra, you can use the crystals as you perform the meditation technique that you learned above. Constant practice is the key to taking advantage of meditation techniques.

Root Chakra
Muladhara

"To be rooted is perhaps the most important and least recognized need for the human soul."

– Simone Weil

This is the 1ˢᵗ Chakra.

Location: Base of the spine

Color Representation: Red

Symbol: Square

Seed Mantra: Lam

Corresponding Organ/Body Parts: Prostate, bladder, kidneys, suprarenal glands, spine

Spinal Pair: Crown Chakra (1/7)

Sense: Smell

Gem: Coral

Planet: Mars

Overflowing: Overly possessive

Lacking: Ungrounded, homeless

Element: Earth

Shakti Manifestation

Stability / Survival / Grounding / Self-Preservation

The 1st Chakra is the seat of your physical vitality and your primary instinct to survive. It is that chakra that helps regulate the mechanisms that keep your physical body alive. The main aspect of this chakra is innocence.

How to Open the Root Chakra

Here is a simple technique that you can energize your legs so you achieve better grounding:

Assume a standing position with your feet about hip apart and the heels slightly wider than the toes. Press your feet down and out, like you are pushing apart the floor tiles with the use of your feet. Inhale while you bend your knees, and exhale when you push down into your feet, all the way through your legs. Repeat these movements until your legs and feet begin to "vibrate". You need constant practice to master this technique so you can do this anytime, anywhere, and whatever you are doing.

Use Crystals

To help open up your *Root Chakra,* you can use these crystals:

Hermatite – Stabilizing and Grounding

Rhodchrosite – Clearing

Black Tourmaline – Healing and Protecting

Red Jasper – Activating

Garnet - Balancing

Smokey Quartz – Healing and Protecting

Red Carnelian – Balancing

*Key Points/Actions Steps

The 1st Chakra is linked to your survival instincts and stability. If you cannot be properly grounded because this chakra is not opened, you become overly possessive and tend to rely on other people for survival. On the other hand, the lack of it results in you getting lost and "homeless".

Use the exercise above to help you open this chakra. You can also choose from the crystals listed to further help you in achieving the right balance you need.

How to Apply What You've Learned?

The point of this book is to give teach you how the 7 Spiritual Chakras work and how you can use it to improve your overall well-being. Being healthy is not just about your physical health, but it should also involve your mental and spiritual health.

Your basic instincts should have to join forces with your thinking and feelings to be able to achieve excellent overall health. Some of the chakras are not always open all the way. These chakras are there since you were born, however, some become over-active and others become totally closed. A sense of balance has to be achieved within these energy centers in order to achieve peace within you. This peace will be emanated into your whole being so you achieve excellent well-being.

The techniques and exercises given to you are simple meditation and exercise techniques that you can easily apply in your daily lives.

There is no way that you can apply these techniques in your daily routine because they are easy to learn and do. Even if you live a fast phased life, you can still find time to perform these exercises.

For instance, you can perform the breathing techniques even when in transient. On your way to the office every morning, you can practice your breathing as you wait on a stoplight or when you get stuck in traffic when you go home from work. If you prefer to travel by subway, it is better, since you can practice while on board the train.

The light and color technique to open the *Third Eye Chakra* can be done almost anytime, you just have be observant. You don't need to look for the sunset every single day because you will see a play of light and colors in your daily commute. Watch how the sun's rays touch the plants on your plant box by your porch or see how sunlight kisses the trees in the park. You see beautiful colors all around, you may have passed them by daily and have not noticed them, now is the time to be mindful and be aware of the world around you.

Awareness and mindfulness are two important "tools" that will help you open your chakras.

With regards to the physical exercises to open your chakras, set at least 30 minutes a day to perform them. Adjust your daily routine to include physical activities. If you have a full schedule every day, why not go to bed early so you can wake up the next morning earlier than usual so you can spare a few minutes to exercise.

It is easy if you just become committed and dedicated. It may be difficult in the beginning but when you get the hang of it, everything will be part of your routine.

How To Overcome Any Fear

It is about time that you reclaim the good life that you once had before you were held as hostage by the crippling type of fear and anxiety. This book presents a revolutionary approach that will take you there in a step-by-step manner!

Did you know that about one-third of the people worldwide are secretly suffering from destructive fears like panic attacks, phobias, worries, and obsessions? These are life-long struggles that they have to deal with throughout their respective lifetimes.

Experts have done a great deal of research through the decades to beat fear and anxiety, but there are only a few efforts to translate these efforts into layman's terms. As a result, people do not really know what exactly to do.

This particular work aims to give readers twenty-five practical, specific, and doable ways to deal with fear and anxiety. Hopefully, by the end of your reading experience, you can say with conviction that you are 100 percent fearless. You can get back that life that you once have again.

1-Get Enough Sleep

"Each night, when I go to sleep, I die. And the next morning, when I wake up, I am reborn."

— Mahatma Gandhi

It begins with how you end your day. Usually, you tend to succumb to fear because your brain and body are not well-rested.

According to research, not having a consistent sleep pattern can entail many serious consequences. So, you should try your best to get as much sleep as you can. The normal sleep cycle for a better new day is about eight hours long. If you get that much sleep, then it will be more likely for you to wake up with a fresher and better outlook in life.

Lack of sleep is found to be a great contributor to stress, anxiety, and irrational fear. Also, it negatively affects a person's physical health. And it works two ways – lack of sleep lead to anxiety attacks and anxiety attacks lead to sleep disruption.

If you are currently feeling anxious, you should do some serious effort to avoid sleep disruption. You need to allocate eight to ten hours to account for difficulty in catching some sleep. Also, you need to free yourself from the thoughts that are giving you stress.

Action Steps/Key Ideas/Tips

*)Rest your brain and body to avoid succumbing to fear and anxiety.

*)Complete at least eight hours of sleep to wake up to a fresher and better new day.

*)Allocate eight to ten hours for sleep alone to account for instances wherein your find it difficult to catch that precious sleep.

2-Put a Smile on your Face

"You'll find that life is still worthwhile, if you just smile."

— Charles Chaplin

Smile can go a really long way. Thought it is only painted on your face, it is one way to penetrate your being all the way to your heart.

More often than not, the tough gets going and the going gets tough. And most of the time, things get out of hand and that can be frustrating. When you are frustrated, you feel the stress. And yes, when you are stressed, that's the time when you feel the fear – fear that you won't be able to deliver, fear that you would be found insufficient and incompetent, and fear that you can't really explain at all.

To avoid further problems, you need to pause for a while and smile. If you find no reason to do so, then find and external reason to justify your smile. It can be your family, or your crush. You can even stream a funny YouTube video. Or smile for no reason at all. It might sound a bit crazy but based on experience; it can make you feel a lot better because it will calm your nerves.

Action Steps/Key Ideas/Tips

*)Remember that a simple smile can brighten up your day.

*)Smile can effectively combat fear, stress, and frustration.

*)Find a reason to smile!

3-Take a Pause because you are Hurt

"Human freedom involves our capacity to pause between the stimulus and response and, in that pause, to choose the one response toward which we wish to throw our weight. The capacity to create ourselves, based upon this freedom, is inseparable from consciousness or self-awareness. (p. 100)"

— Rollo May, The Courage to Create

If you truly understand the dynamics of anxiety, then you can easily translate it using a few words. Those words will be: "Take a pause because you are hurt."

Anxiety is actually a reminder that perhaps, stimuli around you are hurting you too much already to the point that you already need to take a short pause. The most logical step is to stop for a bit and not to stay at that state – staying right there will render you paralyzed. What you need to do is to find where you are hurting to address it appropriately. The level of severity of the hurt is actually directly related to the scope of the damage.

The method and strategy of taking a pause can come in many variations. The following are some of the known ways: having a racing heart, taking a deep and heavy breath, constantly obtaining the feeling of dissociation, and spinning your own thoughts. Feel free to choose whichever you feel to be the most effective. Personalization and customization of ways is something that you should do in order to address anxiety effectively.

Taking a pause is okay because it helps you avoid getting to the peak of anxiety. It is better to stop to address the fears right away rather than suppress it deep within. Suppressing the fear might lead to a much more difficult situation that you can't handle anymore.

Here's the thing. If your problem truly is anxiety, then you have nothing to fear because anxiety itself won't hurt you. It is the actions you take after that might hurt you. So regularly take that pause to check where you are really hurting.

Action Steps/Key Ideas/Tips

*)Take a pause and locate where you are hurting.

*)Employ the strategy to deal with stress that you are most comfortable with.

*)Anxiety, on its own, will not hurt you.

4-Acceptance

*"You couldn't relive your life, skipping the awful parts,
without losing what made it worthwhile. You had to accept
it as a whole--like the world, or the person you loved."*

— Stewart O'Nan, The Odds: A Love Story

Anxiety is something that you need to befriend and make friends with as soon as possible. From time to time, you need to speak to yourself and reflect on your anxiety. You need to constantly reassure yourself and tell yourself that you are truly okay. Listen to your heart and your mind. Pay attention to what your heart is craving for. Pay attention to the issues that matter to you. Find the peace within.

Befriending and making peace with your anxiety will help you to find some proactive ways to address it. On the other hand, suppressing it will only be as good as denying it. By denying its existence, you are allowing it to persist and to grow continuously and exponentially.

The true key to obtaining a real solution for the anxiety problem actually lies with acceptance. If you take longer to persist within your comfort zone, blame other people and external factors for the circumstances that you are facing, the longer it will take you to find the hidden opportunities and solutions to your problem connected to anxiety.

Some spiritual experts, acceptance is one step towards feeling better and being better. Once you accept what you fear, there is a chance that you would cease fearing it. At the very least, the intensity of your fear might be lessened.

As you take the long journey towards accepting something, you will begin to feel a bit better about your life and yourself. If you begin to realize that you have several options available at hand, then you can freely go out of your comfort zone. You can stop grieving about your fate. If you want to outgrow your fear and anxiety, you need to embrace and accept your present circumstances. Also, you can find that there's a lot more to life.

Action Steps/Key Ideas/Tips

*)Befriend, embrace, and accept your anxiety.

*)Get out of your comfort zone and allow yourself to grow.

*)Accept even the darkest aspects of your being so that you can feel better and be better.

5-Declutter

In times of life crisis, whether wild fires or smoldering stress, the first thing I do is go back to basics... am I eating right, am I getting enough sleep, am I getting some physical and mental exercise everyday.

- Edward Albert

Physical clutter is a manifestation of a deeper problem. It can be a sign of fear and anxiety piling up in your heart and in your mind. For example, if your workplace is a mess, then you might find it difficult to take some short breaks. It will also make you feel like the work that you have seems not to end. It will somewhat feed your fears within because you are swimming into your stress. So, you need to take fifteen short minutes every day to tidy up a bit your home or your work area.

A clean work place and a clean home is not only an organized space; it is also a space that tends to drive away stress, fear, and anxiety. It will help you think in a more logical manner. Rationality usually takes over an organized workspace.

Again, if clutter at home or at the workplace can mean something more serious, then what should be done? To avoid the ill effects of excessive clutter, you will need to keep an eye on your day-to-day affairs. For example, you need to keep everything within the manageable level.

According to experts, the clutter around you can make you constantly distracted. It will also somewhat weigh you down because you will feel less confident about yourself. Disorderliness leads to having less accomplishments and it leads to lower level of self-esteem. When you are not accomplishing enough, you tend to question your capability and you also have the tendency to dread what is coming in the future.

To move forward, inevitably, you need to reduce the clutter in order to cut down the level of stress that can be caused by it. If you will be able to do this properly, you will get the most amazing of rewards, namely: a very attractive place of abode, a significantly lowered level of stress, and a more organized and highly productive kind of life.

But of course, you need to begin with the most basic things: you have to declutter you house, your place of work, and of course, your life.

Action Steps/Key Ideas/Tips

*)Cut down the clutter because it will lead to higher level of productivity.

*)A more organized living and working space will help you think clearly.

*)Decluttering your life only takes at least fifteen minutes per day.

6-Show Gratitude

"Cultivate the habit of being grateful for every good thing that comes to you, and to give thanks continuously. And because all things have contributed to your advancement, you should include all things in your gratitude."

— Ralph Waldo Emerson

Be thankful and never be afraid to show how grateful you are. Based on research, expressing your gratitude is helpful in reducing the levels of anxiety because it helps a person become better rested. If you wish, you may start making a journal of gratitude to have a detailed recording of what you should be thankful for in life. This will help you maintain the mindset of being appreciative and at the same time, a gratitude journal will keep you from being overwhelmed.

Bearing an extremely comparative mindset will not only take away your capability to be thankful; it will also heighten your anxiety levels. Basically, the real issue here is maintaining an unhealthy level of fear in your lifestyle because you are not certain of what's going to happen in the future. As one becomes too focused on what's yet to happen in the future, you tend to ignore what has already been given in your life. Therefore, you are robbing yourself of the opportunity to relax and enjoy what's happening at present.

This builds up the fear because paranoia is somewhat reinforced by paranoia. The structure is somewhat like a spiral and it seems not to end. Inside the very depths of your consciousness, you tend to fight it by explaining to yourself how foolish it is to dwell on worry and in fear. However, your heart tends to swim into fear and you remain in the state of being afraid. Indeed, it is impossible to control what's going to happen tomorrow and your spirit struggle because you aim to gain control of everything and anything. And yes, sad to say, this is a pointless endeavor.

In the end, anxiety and fear holds you back from showing how thankful you are. As a corollary, gratitude is one of the most important tools to fight fear and corollary. In the end, you need to let the thankfulness flow and express it consciously so that your focus will not be on the future but in present-day concerns. Live your life one day at a time and you will enjoy it more. All your fears will become smaller than what they used to be and peace will endure in your life.

Action Steps/Key Ideas/Tips

*)Do not be afraid to show how thankful you are for everything.

*)Gratitude is the best weapon against fear and anxiety.

*)Live your life one day at a time. Focus at the present and not in the future.

7-Eat the Right Stuff

"The food you eat can be either the safest and most powerful form of medicine or the slowest form of poison."

— Ann Wigmore

Fear and anxiety is capable of putting your body out of its usual dynamic functions. The manifestations are the following: either you will lose your usual appetite, your preferences in food might drastically change, or you might even end up craving particular food. But in order to support the needs of your body, you will have to put some serious effort to provide your body with its basic nutritional requirements, like vitamin B rich food for your brain and omega-3 for your blood vessels. You also need to take in sufficient carbohydrate rich food for energy.

According to studies, intake of vitamin B will help you have a more stable mental health. On the other hand, omega 3 complex in your diet can help significantly decrease anxiety and depression symptoms. Also, if you will take in the right kind of carbohydrates, especially those that come from whole grains, you will find yourself feeling better because of the neurotransmitters that regulate serotonin. It will also help you feel calm. Even if you are consistently craving for sweets and foods that are processed, you need to try your best to suppress it because according to research, it will only increase anxiety symptoms.

You need to watch what you eat. According to a published study in a Psychiatry Journal in the US, eating habits are directly correlated to anxiety and depression of women. For women who were into the western type of diet, they tend to be more anxious and depressed than the women who were into the traditional type of diet. The Western diet consists of beer, refined grains, sweets, processed food, and fast food.

On the other hand, the traditional type of diet usually consists of fruits, veggies, fish, meat, and whole grains.

Also, there are certain types of food that successfully improve the mood of people. Among these are bananas, poultry, oats, milk, nuts, peanut butter, sesame seeds, and peanut butter. You might be wondering how these are able to do it. They have one common component: tryptophan. Tryptophan helps in producing serotonin. And as mentioned earlier, this neurotransmitter is a feel good substance that makes you feel calm and happy.

Finally, you need to know that caffeine and alcohol are triggers of anxiety of depression. You do not need to eliminate these substances completely – they serve a certain purpose to your diet; however, you need to cut down your consumption by fifty percent. Slowly and gradually, over a ten-day period, you must try reducing alcohol and caffeine intake by at least ten percent daily.

Many people who are depressed turn to alcohol to "drown" their sadness. However, this is a wrong move since processed alcohol only leads to symptoms that are very much similar to anxiety.

On the other hand, caffeine only heightens the level of anxiety because it negatively affects the pattern of sleep. The importance of sleep in combatting your anxiety has already been discussed in an earlier chapter. By now, you already know that irregular sleep pattern only induce further fear and anxiety.

Action Steps/Key Ideas/Tips

*)Take in sufficient amounts of Vitamin B and omega 3.

*)For carbohydrate sources, go for whole grain.

*)Cut down your intake of caffeine and alcohol because these can worsen your condition.

8-Meditate

"Meditation is a mysterious method of self-restoration. It involves "shutting" out the outside world, and by that means sensing the universal "presence" which is, incidentally, absolute perfect peace. It is basically an existential "time-out"—a way to "come up for a breath of air" out of the noisy clutter of the world. But don't be afraid, there is nothing arcane or supernatural or creepy about the notion of taking a time-out. Ball players do it. Kids do it, when prompted by their parents. Heck, even your computer does it (and sometimes not when you want it to). So, why not you? A meditation can be as simple as taking a series of easy breaths, and slowly, gently counting to ten in your mind."

— Vera Nazarian, The Perpetual Calendar of Inspiration

At this point, there is a need to define what meditation truly is. Yes, you may have an idea that it is a well-known relaxation method, but science tells us that it is much more than that. Through a series of research, it was found out that meditation actually leads to the increase in the brain's grey matter. In simplified terms, meditation finds a way to rewire the body so that it will feel less stress for putting the same amount of effort. In the end, it shields you from feeling fear and anxiety.

In much more recent research efforts, it was suggested that meditation has a good effect of brain activity. It can control mood, stress, and anxiety. Since it is relaxing, meditation can help in blocking thoughts that can provoke your fears and anxiety.

However, there is a proper way of doing meditation. If you do it right, you will find rest and you will even feel energized and renewed. Proper meditation can bring about rest and it can dissolve your anxiety and stress. Your body has the innate capability to take care of stress while you sleep. However, if you are not able to get enough rest, stress and insomnia might ensue.

If you wish to combat stress and anxiety, you might want to choose TM or transcendental meditation. This is a technique that is proven scientifically to provide the body one of the deepest known state of rest and relaxation. It can bring about coherence to your brain waves. Within a cycle of twenty minutes worth of meditation, you will find yourself more alert. Also, fatigue and stress would be instantly reduced. According to research, transcendental meditation can give you peacefulness and calmness.

Action Steps/Key Ideas/Tips

*)Proper meditation can increase your brain's grey matter.

*)Meditation has a good effect on the activity of brain.

*)Doing meditation right can bring about calmness and peacefulness.

9-Get Involved in Physical Activities

"Exercises are like prose, whereas yoga is the poetry of movements. Once you understand the grammar of yoga; you can write your poetry of movements."

— Amit Ray, Yoga and Vipassana: An Integrated Life Style

Getting physical – this is one of the most enjoyable ways of fighting your number one fear. By getting more involved in physical activities, you will become more fit and healthy. Your body functions will normalize. The most desirable effect of physical activities is that your levels of anxiety would be reduced. According to evidence, it can be concluded that anxiety levels can be reduced significantly by doing more exercise.

To be more specific, there are preferred exercise routine that can help reduce fear and anxiety, among these are: (1) swimming, running, and biking, among other aerobic exercise routines; and (2) long term programs of exercise (those that take at least twelve to fifteen weeks to complete) rather than those that are short. Also, it was found out that people who are out of shape derive more benefit from exercise than those who are already fit. Lastly, experiments suggest that those people who have high level of anxiety levels tend to benefit more from getting involved from physical activities than those who have little or no anxiety.

It was recommended by a series of studies that a person should get involved in at least half an hour of moderate exercise every single day if you want to reap the maximum benefit of getting physical. Increasing the intensity of your exercise routines will not hurt either. In fact, there are separate studies attesting to the fact that it can be helpful in making you feel better about yourself.

To summarize, the best results can be derived if exercise will be done with proper diet and meditation, both of which have been discussed already in earlier chapters of this compendium.

Action Steps/Key Ideas/Tips

*)Exercise and physical activities will help you normalize the different important functions of your body.

*)Get involved in exercise routines that are aerobic; also, try going for exercise programs that last for twelve to fifteen weeks.

*)Do your exercise simultaneously with proper diet and the right kind of meditation.

10-Use Your Lungs

"Slow, deep breathing is a powerful anti-stress technique. When you bring air down into the lower portion of the lungs, where the oxygen exchange is most efficient, heart rate slows, blood pressure decreases, muscles relax, anxiety eases and the mind calms."

– Carol Krucoff

Experts say that people of today have forgotten how to use their lungs properly. This is especially true for people who live in the West and to those who are exposed to a highly industrialized society. Therefore, people are actually stuck in the wrong way of breathing. They never realize that this is dovetailed by muscles that are tense and increased rate of respiration. We forget the true definition of relaxation because we forgot how to use our lungs properly. And we often expose our lungs to pollutants that lead to a deteriorated state of health.

In order to be reminded how to do the proper breathing, one needs to look at a baby. Babies are known to breathe from their bellies. However, as people age, they shift to a wrong method – the shallow type of breathing that only reaches the chest.

Breathing is important in combatting stress and anxiety because it is one of the many body functions that can be both done unconsciously and consciously. According to studies, doing a focused type of breathing can lead to reduced anxiety and stress. It can also improve the disposition of menopausal women. For women who are in pain due to PMS, focused breathing can bring remedy as well.

In breathing, one has to take in as much air as possible. This will help you take in as much oxygen that is needed and take out as much carbon dioxide out of the system. The exchange of gases will help you become a healthier individual.

So what should be done in order to master proper breathing techniques and combat anxiety? First, you need to make sure that you are not exposed to pollutants. Next, try breathing deeply – if you can feel that the air is reaching your navel, then you are doing it right. Then, you need to improve your body's posture. Lastly, try to repeat the proper breathing pattern so that you will be able to adopt the technique even when you are unconscious.

Action Steps/Key Ideas/Tips

*)Use your lungs properly to combat the fear.

*)Make sure to avoid pollutants.

*)If the air you are breathing in can be felt around your navel, then you are doing it right.

11-Reflect on your Thoughts

"Given enough time, you could convince yourself that loneliness was something better, that it was solitude, the ideal condition for reflection, even a kind of freedom.

Once you were thus convinced, you were foolish to open the door and let anyone in, not all the way in. You risked the hard-won equilibrium, that tranquility that you called peace."

— Dean Koontz, The Good Guy

According to an expert, when people are filled with anxiety, they tend to have ideas that are out of this world. They tend to believe these ideas no matter how unrealistic and improbable for them to occur. These only lead to a heightened level of anxiety in an individual.

For example, because you fear the fact that you are not going to make it on time, you will be led by your brain to believe that you will be fired from your job. According to experts, you need to take a short pause and reflect on what's going on in your head. Which of the things that you are thinking are reasonable and worth believing? Which ones are meant to distract you?

Answering the following questions will help you facilitate the process of reflection:

(1) How realistic is this thing I am worrying about?

(2) How likely are my worries bound to happen?

(3) How difficult will it be to bear the worst possible condition?

(4) What can I do to improve the situation? Am I really that helpless?

(5) Is there anything that I can do to prepare for the worst of situations?

Action Steps/Key Ideas/Tips

*)People who are anxious tend to think of outlandish possibilities.

*)Never dive into the most out-of-this-world type of situations. They are not likely to happen.

*)Ask yourself reflective questions and try to act as reasonably as possible to conquer the fear.

12-Write Down Everything

"Those who find ugly meanings in beautiful things are corrupt without being charming. This is a fault. Those who find beautiful meanings in beautiful things are the cultivated. For these there is hope. They are the elect to whom beautiful things mean only Beauty."

— Oscar Wilde, The Picture of Dorian Gray

Writing your fears on a piece of paper is an effective way to contain them. Also, when you write them down, you tend to find it easier to acknowledge that you have those kinds of fear. Remember, denying their existence won't help you at all; acceptance is actually the first step for you to go back to the light.

Writing down your fears help you externalize the fear that you have within. It helps you uncover the fears that tend to lurk at the darkest depths of your head. By writing your fears, you tend to have the sense of control. And in the process, you seem to pluck out each from your system.

If you want, you can shred the paper into pieces. Or you can symbolically burn the piece of paper. For others, they prefer posting it on their corkboard as a reminder of what their enemies are. Choose the method that works for you.

Others keep a "fear journal" to document all their fears. For others, they also write down the remedy that was effective in shooting down a particular fear. This way, they remind themselves of methods that work.

Action Steps/Key Ideas/Tips

*)Writing is an effective means to acknowledge the existence of your fears.

*)Writing down your fear will help you "pluck out" negativities from the deepest and darkest parts of your being.

*)Keep a fear journal to document your fears.

13-Plan Ahead

"How would your life be different if...you had a plan of action towards your goals? Let today be the day...You stop allowing your days to be stolen by busy nothingness and take calculated steps towards your goals."

— Steve Maraboli, The Power of One

Anxiety – or any problem for that matter – can be fought effectively if you plan ahead of time. You can try to make a to-do list or a schedule to make your life more structured. This will increase your level of productivity. When that happens, you will become more confident about yourself, you will feel less stress, and you will have fewer reasons to fear. By convincing yourself that you are prepared well enough, you can start forgetting about beliefs that produce fear and anxiety.

You need to plan way ahead of time. In order to cope up better with anxiety, you need to master the art of managing your time. Therefore, you need to learn how to set your goals and align them accordingly and systematically. That way, you know exactly what's coming. Remember that you are lucky because technology is by your side. It is much easier to make a schedule because you can use gadgets and apps to take care of the details for you.

Also, you will have fewer reasons to fear what's coming when you set your priorities right. If you know that you are doing the most important things first, you can be confident that you are doing things right. By making a priority list that indicates the corresponding deadlines, you can be constantly reminded of what needs to be done.

Your life will be better if you know how to manage your time. You will have less reason to fear if you devote a portion of your time planning ahead. We usually fear what's coming if we do not orient ourselves of what the future has in store for us. Prepare a schedule and adhere to it strictly. But never forget to schedule breaks in between, too.

Action Steps/Key Ideas/Tips

*)Plan how you will attack your fear.

*)Keep a well-structured schedule.

*)Create a priority list.

14-Face Change

"Here's to the crazy ones. The misfits. The rebels. The troublemakers. The round pegs in the square holes. The ones who see things differently. They're not fond of rules. And they have no respect for the status quo. You can quote them, disagree with them, glorify or vilify them. About the only thing you can't do is ignore them. Because they change things. They push the human race forward. And while some may see them as the crazy ones, we see genius. Because the people who are crazy enough to think they can change the world, are the ones who do."

— Apple Inc.

Most of us feel the fear because we do not want change. This leads to a situation wherein we tend to swim against the current and that can consume us completely.

Whenever there is an impending change, think first of the basics. Fear and anxiety are two of the emotions that can lead to paralysis. It can play tricks on your mind and it never fails to strike you when you least need it. If you want to think clearly and calmly, you have to face change with all the courage that you can muster.

The first thing that you can do is to demystify the impending change. Tell yourself that whenever something is bound to change, it is natural to feel fear and anxiety. But you must not allow fear and anxiety to take over and dominate. When properly regulated, fear is likely to disappear with time.

Allow yourself to feel the fear. Experts even suggest people to "feel the fear" because it is just a normal part of the cycle. Remember that even the most courageous people feel anxious at times. This will make you feel human.

You will suffer less if you will not suppress your anxiety. Let it go! It will help if you allow yourself to fee it and at the same time, couple it with some positive thinking.

Do not hide your real emotions. Express it every single time you can. Suppressed emotions can only lead to the wreckage of both your body and your mind.

Remember, emotions and feelings come in and come out like waves. If you are anxious of changes, you need to put your fullest focus on current waves. Again, let it go.

Action Steps/Key Ideas/Tips

*)Demystify the fear of change.

*)Let yourself feel the fear; never suppress it.

*)Express your feelings whenever there's a chance. Let it go!

15-Keep your Hands Full

"Being busy is better than being bored. Bored left a long time ago. Busy is always around for me."

— Tabitha Robin

Whenever you feel anxious, it is always a great option to keep your hands full. That way, you tend to channel your attention to activities that are meaningful and directed by goals. Experts even suggest that you deal with activities that you can do and make you feel like you are not feeling any fear or anxiety at all.

If you are anxious and you have to iron your clothes, proceed with what you have to do. If you are fearful but you have to watch a movie, go ahead. If you are anxious and you need to buy something at the grocery, proceed anyway.

When you are struck by anxiety, the worst thing that you can choose to do is to remain still. Being passive will only remind you of the reasons of your fear. The reasons tend to grow out of proportion – they might eat you up without your knowing.

By doing the things that you need to accomplish will help you understand and learn life's key lessons. Living life as if you don't fear even when you are really anxious will help you get by day after day and task after task.

Action Steps/Key Ideas/Tips

*)Keep your hands full to channel your attention to activities that are meaningful and goal-directed.

*)Proceed with your day-to-day affairs even if you are filled with anxiety.

*)Choosing to be passive and remaining still is an unwise choice because it will only make your fears grow out of proportion.

16-Do Some Positive Talk to Yourself

"Keep your thoughts positive because your thoughts become your words. Keep your words positive because your words become your behavior. Keep your behavior positive because your behavior becomes your habits. Keep your habits positive because your habits become your values. Keep your values positive because your values become your destiny."

— Mahatma Gandhi

Thinking positively will help you manage stress and fight off fears and anxiety. However, if you are the type who tends to practice negative self-talk, you must make it a point to unlearn this unhealthy practice.

Always ask yourself: Do you perceive as glass as something that is half-full or half-empty? True, this question has already been asked, perhaps decades or centuries ago, but the essence and the significance remains. By testing yourself if you are an optimist or a pessimist, then the proper course of actions to overcome fears will be easier to address.

There are related studies wherein it has been established that pessimism and optimism can bring about many effects on a person's health and physical state. But more than that, it has a great effect of a persons' point of view. The way they contain fear is greatly affected by this. Positive thinking can help in the effective facilitation of management of stress. Consequently, it can also help in controlling one's fears. On the other hand, pessimists tend to give in to their fears.

Remember, you need to do some positive self-talk in order to reinforce the value of optimism. By doing a positive thinking, one does not necessarily have to ignore the bad things happening around you. Instead, positive thinking teaches individuals to do things in the most productive and positive ways despite the unpleasant situation. You are trained to think that the best can happen despite all the adversities.

Positive thought are often borne out of positive self-talk. Positive self-talk is like a limitless stream of thoughts that are not spoken. They usually run and go on inside your head. For pessimistic people, the stream of thought is usually negative. But for optimists, they choose to keep their self-talk positive at all times.

Remember, if the thoughts are negative, you invite negative situations to occur. You justify the existence of your fears by feeding them so that they will be larger than life.

According to research, aside from successfully beating anxiety, there are may benefits that can be derived from positive self-talk. The following are just some of the examples: significant increase in a person's life span, lowered rate of depression, reduced level of distress, higher resistance against flu and colds, improved physical and psychological welfare and well-being, reduced level of death due to heart attack, and improved skills in coping up during stress and hardships.

Action Steps/Key Ideas/Tips

*)Positive self-talk can help fight off stress, fears, and anxiety.

*)Optimism teaches individuals to be productive and happy despite adversity.

*)Positive self-talk can bring about better physical, mental, and psychological health.

17-Be Mindful at All Times

Many misunderstand mindfulness as a notion or a clever idea that can be applied directly, but unfortunately things aren't as simple as that. Rather, mindfulness is a skill – a way of controlling your attention – that can be improved over time with continuous daily training.

– Jacob Piet

Mindfulness is an effective tool to stop rumination and worrying. This involves a process of putting into use the non-judgmental type of awareness to present or express one's emotions and thoughts. It serves as a strategy in the cognitive and behavioral therapy.

According to studies, mindfulness can help in beating fear and anxiety because it encourages people to change their style of thinking. Also, they are expected to disengage from worry and rumination as a method of emotional response. With mindfulness, people tend to dwell on thinking of more specific and more concrete methods of finding solutions. Experts call this phenomenon as the cognitive restructure thinking. This encourages a more positive approach of thinking.

Mindfulness, however, should not be misunderstood as a method of coming up with direct solutions to complicated problems. Be warned, however, that things are not that simple. Instead, mindfulness should be thought of as a technique or a skill. It is a strategy to control your attention and this can be improved by training daily and continuously.

By doing a systematic training of mindfulness, you can significantly improve the manner by which you handle your anxiety. Even patients of depression are helped out by mindfulness techniques.

Action Steps/Key Ideas/Tips

*)Mindfulness helps restructure the way by which you think.

*)Mindfulness techniques encourage a positive thinking approach.

*)By training daily, consistently, and continuously, you can improve your strategy.

18-Revisit the Victories that you Have Collected

"Never do a single thing in the anticipation to prove something to someone who has hurt you. If someone has hurt or offended you (whoever that person may be), never perform anything or strive for anything in your life with the mind of proving something to that someone/ to those people. May nothing that you do be done with any thought of them in mind. There is nothing that needs to be proven."

— C. JoyBell C.

Remember your past victories because they will help you realize your self-worth. Victory represents a moment in your lifetime wherein you have proven yourself worthy of something great. It can be a proof of superiority or capability to survive. If you have problems with fears and anxiety, you need to remember your past victories and you feel a lot better.

Celebrate and reflect on your victories because it shows your uniqueness and it will be a great means to release the tensions within. It leads you to a higher level of consciousness.

Victory is embedded in your mind in the same way that anxiety can conquer your being. They are actually things that are maintained in your consciousness. To fight off anxiety, therefore, it would be logical to suggest that victories can be the best way to counter these negative thoughts. It will make you remember that you are worthy because once in your life, you were able to win a certain battle.

Action Steps/Key Ideas/Tips

*)Victories will help you realize your self-worth.

*)Use victories to fight your anxieties.

*)Victories can lead you to a higher level of consciousness.

19-Hang Out with Friends

"Piglet sidled up to Pooh from behind. "Pooh?" he whispered.

"Yes, Piglet?"

"Nothing," said Piglet, taking Pooh's hand. "I just wanted to be sure of you."

— *A.A. Milne, Winnie-the-Pooh*

Hanging out with friends will be a great help to ease the tension brought about by fear, stress, anger, and anxiety.

If you are facing any problem, what do you do? People tend to tell their problems to their most trusted friends. This way, any problem becomes much easier to bear. Any difficulty seems to be more manageable. The same is true when it comes to anxiety. If you fear something, tell your most trusted friends. For sure, they will be willing to help.

Oftentimes, friends try their best to help. Real friends will be willing to go with you wherever you want to go just to make sure that you are doing fine and that you are always safe. If they know that a friend fears anything, they will not leave them alone. They will make sure that the person has somebody to talk to. This is already a great help for a fearful person.

Also, good friends will make sure that you are taking the necessary medications and that you are following the "rules" that will help improve your condition. Friends will also make sure that you are always kept out of danger and that you find your way out of the fearful situation. They will suggest fun activities like strolling around or watching a good movie to help you feel better.

In the end, good friends will make you feel assured. They will also make you realize that things are a lot better if you have somebody who understands to share them with.

Finally, friends will make you understand that fear should be regulated. And if you succeed with such regulation, you will find out that it is your body's coping mechanism.

Action Steps/Key Ideas/Tips

*)Find good friends to share your situation with.

*)Good friends will not leave you alone. They will always keep you safe.

*)Friends will help you realize that it is completely normal to fear for as long as you learn to control your fears again.

20-Making a Fear Ladder

"I must not fear. Fear is the mind-killer. Fear is the little-death that brings total obliteration. I will face my fear. I will permit it to pass over me and through me. And when it has gone past I will turn the inner eye to see its path. Where the fear has gone there will be nothing. Only I will remain."

— Frank Herbert, Dune

This technique is simple. You can list down places, situations, and objects that you are anxious of. For instance, if you are afraid of cats, you may include any of the following: looking at photographs of cats, sitting beside cats, seeing a cat by the window, being approached by a cat, or hearing a cat meow. On the other hand, if you fear to be with people, then you might write down: saying hello to your boss, going to a party, asking a question to a complete stranger, answering a phone call, talking with the saleslady, among others.

Here's the next step: you need to group similar fears together. If you have more than one fear, you need to do this. You need to decide on your theme to have a basis for grouping. For example, you can group your fears as "living things" and "non-living things." Once you are done making a list, you need to arrange the things on the list from the least fearful to the most fearful. You can use a rating scale to help you arrange your fear ladder.

While you make your fear ladder, you will find out that it becomes easier for you to point out your goals. Ask yourself: What exactly do you want to do after doing the fear ladder? What do you wish to achieve?

For each theme, you need to build a separate ladder. For each ladder, you have to express a specific goal. This way, you get to know your fears better. Also, you will know which of your fears are easier to address. From there, you can make a plan of action. If you feel that it is needed, you may ask help from other people.

Action Steps/Key Ideas/Tips

*)List down your fears and organize them according to theme to point out similar ones.

*)Arrange the fears according to the level of fear that you feel for each.

*)Create end goals that you wish to achieve upon addressing the fears in the fear ladder.

21-Get Support from Family

*"Family is family, and is not determined by marriage
certificates, divorce papers, and adoption documents.
Families are made in the heart. The only time family
becomes null is when those ties in the heart are cut. If you
cut those ties, those people are not your family. If you
make those ties, those people are your family. And if you
hate those ties, those people will still be your family
because whatever you hate will always be with you."*

— C. JoyBell C.

Whenever you have a problem, be it physical or emotional, it is always difficult to sort it out alone. It is always easier to face any difficulty when you know that someone sympathizes with your situation. This way, the unpleasant things can be better understood. However, people around us won't always hand over the sympathy that we need. There are times when they can only offer ridicule or shame.

In such situations, you will appreciate having family members around. The same situation is true when you are facing anxiety or fear. It is not healthy to keep it secret, but it won't be healthy if you will share it with people who will not understand because they will only bring your shame and ridicule. If you have anxiety problems, the best people to tell are those within your family. They offer unconditional love and support. They will help you calm down and they will show you the way out of your situation. Family members usually believe you even if they do not fully understand. They are the people whom you can expect not to exert the unnecessary pressure to be okay. Your fear will be less fearful because you know that you are no longer alone.

When you are struggling with your fear or anxiety problem, or when you are too stressed out, you have to tell it to the people closest to you. This way, you tend to understand yourself better. You have the opportunity to dissect the origins of your fears. Suddenly, you feel that solution is just around the corner. Little by little, you can feel that things are getting a bit better and problems appear to have solutions.

Choose a family member to be your confidant. They won't judge you. They may not understand, but they will remain loyal to you through thick and thin. They also have the genuine concern, and they will help you out sincerely to bring down your fear. You do not have to face all of these challenges alone.

Action Steps/Key Ideas/Tips

*)Do not face the fear or anxiety problem alone.

*)Find someone who will sincerely sympathize.

*)Family members may not always understand, but they will always believe you.

22-Relax your Breathing

"Just breathing can be such a luxury sometimes."

— Walter Kirn, Up in the Air

Not everyone is given the privilege to breath freely and easily. You need to enjoy this privilege to the fullest, and you will be surprised because it can help you fight your fears and anxiety.

Try to practice your deep breathing exercises regularly. You have to find a spot where you won't be disturbed by anyone. As much as possible, that place should be quiet – quiet enough so that you can hear your own breathing. In the process, you might need to loosen up your clothing and remove the tight ones. This will help you feel as comfortable as possible.

Find your most comfortable chair. Make sure that you will support your head properly. Or you can choose to lie down on a bed or on the floor. Put your hands on the side with your palms facing up. If you choose to lie down, try to stretch your legs out in such a way that you keep them apart. If you are sitting on a chair, by all means, do not cross your legs because it might hamper free breathing.

For better breathing, you need to relax. Try to do this as slowly as possible and find your regular and natural rhythm. These steps will help you calm down:

(1) Fill your lungs with all the air that you can take in. Be careful not to force air in. Try to fill your lungs from the bottom.

(2) When taking in air, use your nose. When breathing out, use your mouth.

(3) Try to breathe in as slowly as possible. To make it regular, try to count from one to five while completing the breathing cycle. In the beginning, you will notice that it is difficult to reach five.

(4) Do the same for breathing out.

(5) Try to do this repeatedly until you calm your nerves. Continue breathing without any pause. As much as possible, do not hold your breath back.

Relaxed breathing should be done from 3 to 5 minutes, at least three times a day. If you are stressed or anxious, doing this more often might help.

Action Steps/Key Ideas/Tips

*)Find a quiet place wherein you can hear yourself breathing.

*)Try to catch up with your natural and regular breathing rhythm.

*)Practice relaxed breathing at least three times a day to make you feel better.

23-Relax your Muscles

"Rather was it not a series of seven uneasy days, spent in restless pursuit of pleasure, and a wearisome anxiety to find out how to make the most of them? Where was the quiet, where the promised rest?"

— Charles Lamb

Believe it or not, this technique will only take twenty minutes of your time. All you need to do is stretch some of your muscle groups and bring them back to their relaxed state. This way, you will successfully release all the tension that you are hiding inside your body. The relaxation of the body and the relaxation of your mind will soon follow.

Here's what you should do: First, you need to find your favorite spot – preferably one that is quiet and warm. That place should have no distractions. Then, you can sit or lie down there. You need to close your eyes and start to focus on your breathing – trying to do it as slowly and as deeply as you can.

Identify your aching muscles. Focus on those muscles longer and spend time in relaxing them. Then, to help you in relaxing further, you might want to play your favorite music. It should be the soothing kind of music, not the distracting type. Note that there are different groups of muscles that you need to focus on:

(1) **Facial muscles**: There is a need to push the eyebrows in such a way that they will meet each other. The resulting facial expression is similar to that of frowning. After that, you may release.

(2) **Neck muscles**: Tilt your head gently forwards. Then, push your chin downwards towards the chest and lift it slowly again.

(3) **Shoulder muscles**: Pull each of your shoulder towards the corresponding ear and then try to relax them as you move each along the direction of the corresponding foot.

(4) **Chest muscles**: Try to breathe as slowly as possible and make sure that you are feeling your diaphragm. This is located just below the bottom rib. This way, you can be sure that you are utilizing your entire lungs. Try to breath out slowly and allow your belly to deflate until all the air inside your lungs is released.

(5) **Arm muscles**: Try to stretch each of your arms away from your body. Reach for the farthest point you can for a few seconds, and then relax.

(6) **Leg muscles**: Push each of your toes away from your body and then pull each of them towards your body. Now, try to relax.

(7) **Wrist muscles**: Try to stretch each of your wrists by trying to pull each of your hand up towards your direction. Then, gently pull each of your fingers. After this, you are ready to relax your wrist.

Do the entire routine using as much time as you need. More importantly, try doing these while your eyes are closed so that you can find peace with yourself.

Action Steps/Key Ideas/Tips

*)Relaxing your muscle will only take at least 20 minutes of your time.

*)Spend more time relaxing your aching muscles.

*)Focus on the seven muscle groups to get the best results.

24-Transform your Fears into Inspirations

"If you're reading this...

Congratulations, you're alive.

If that's not something to smile about,

then I don't know what is."

— Chad Sugg, Monsters Under Your Head

In order to beat your fears, you need to find a way to transform them into inspiration. To help you out, there are at least four methods to successfully transform your fears into sources of inspiration:

(1) Live in the simplest manner possible. If you are not familiar about the minimalist type of lifestyle, you can start researching about that now. In essence, it will help you to go back to basics. It will teach you not to hold on to material stuff. By leading a simple kind of life, you will have less reason to fear.

(2) Write down everything. Oftentimes, when your mind is filled with ideas —be it bright or dull – you are too afraid that you might lose them all. Never trust your rusty memory! Write everything down so that you can free up your brain. You can keep a notepad and a pen in your car, in your bedroom, and in the office. Or you can use your mobile device to do this successfully.

(3) Chill! A body filled with anxiety is a body that lacks relaxation and rest. There are techniques that you can subscribe to in order to improve your sleep and relaxation regimen. The best news is that most of them are free.

(4) Change your mental habits and the way you view things. There are habits that keep you stuck to your fears and anxiety. The way you think can improve the way you view your life.

In order to transform your fears into inspiration, you need to be at ease with yourself. However, many people say that they are too busy to be at ease. This is a problem because one has to be truly willing before positive results can be obtained. But you can never too busy if you truly want to turn your life around. If your life is bound to change for the better, then you have to do whatever it takes. And yes, most of the time, techniques usually take only a few minutes to change the way you think. And the techniques are not complicated at all.

Have an open mind. And changing anxiety or fears into inspiration involves many steps, but it begins with having an open mind. This will help you find your way out of anxiety and living an inspire life.

You have to consciously guide your mind to move away from unskillful and counter-productive emotions like fear, anger, and anxiety. You need to find a way to replace these with cheerfulness and kindness – these are the key to real happiness.

Action Steps/Key Ideas/Tips

*)Live simply in order to appreciate what truly matters in your life.

*)Keep an open mind. This is the beginning of learning the techniques of turning your fears into inspiration.

*)Replace your fear, anger and anxiety with cheerfulness and kindness. This will help you become truly happy.

25-Dream On and Dream Big

"Hold fast to dreams,

For if dreams die

Life is a broken-winged bird,

That cannot fly."

— Langston Hughes

More often than not, your source of fear and anxiety might resemble any of the following:

(1) I failed doing the same thing when I attempted to do it a long time ago.

(2) I am fearful of what other people might be saying about my status and I once I decide to quit this job.

(3) It is fearful to give up the current lifestyle that I am currently enjoying.

(4) This job bores me a lot but I do not have the confidence that I have sufficient skills and talents in beginning anew in another career path.

(5) It feels like I am trapped in the job that I currently have and I feel uncertain about the possibility of getting out of here without hurting myself.

(6) I am truly fearful of the consequences of the actions that I would take should I follow my heart.

According to research, if you can relate to any or all of these fears, then you are in a situation wherein your fears are in control of your life.

In the process, you block the opportunities that truly belong to you, and you are saying no to new blessings because you doubt your own talents, skills, and capabilities. Remember, success comes in different forms. There are no standard forms of success. Also, missions and passions come in varied shapes and sizes. So there's nothing wrong in dreaming on and dreaming big. You have an amazing set of talents and skills.

For instance, your life mission is to truly inspire other people by means of following what your heart is yearning for. And in the process of following your dreams, you need to utilize other techniques that were already discussed in earlier chapters of this book like writing, coaching, meditation, and yoga. Also, feel free to talk with other people. Communicate your dreams and aspirations. Dreams and aspirations, when communicated with others have better chances of coming true.

Be your best every day. And by saying "best," remember that you do not have to subscribe to a single definition or notion of what is best. Of course, you can use varied techniques in doing so.

Below are a series of steps that you can try to better own your dream and aspirations. It will help you better appreciate the warrior within and in combatting your worst fears:

(1) Write your twenty strengths and associate each of these to a specific emotion.

(2) Write your fears that you usually block as you move along with your life. Associate each of the fears with a specific emotion.

(3) Take a look at the list that you were able to come up with. Now, try framing your fears again with due consideration to the strengths that you have listed down.

(4) In order to reach your dreams and aspirations, what things do you need to add or take away from your life so that you can be more victorious every single day?

Chase your happiness today! Dream on and dream big. Many people find themselves frustrated because they held themselves back. Never surrender your dreams to your fears. You are a resilient person who can come up with creative solutions to your anxiety and fear problems.

Be happy because you are truly worth it.

Action Steps/Key Ideas/Tips

*)Don't hold your fears back just because you are afraid of the repercussions of your actions.

*)Get to know your strengths and weaknesses and use your knowledge to improve the way you view yourself and your dreams.

*)Never subscribe to a single definition of "success."

Final Thoughts

Anxiety is something that is prevalent in our modern society. It has already reached a point wherein everyone is a potential victim and they might not even know about it. It truly is a negative experience and the levels or intensity may vary. If you are struggling with fear and anxiety, you might feel that you are helpless. It might even feel like it would be impossible for you to overcome it. But here's the good news: there are physical and mental options in order to reduce fear and anxiety levels. These are discussed fully in this compendium. This book will help you point out anxiety right at its source. If you recently struggled with fear and anxiety attack, you need to fight it right away by identifying the root of the problem. This book will help you answer the following questions:

*) Can you identify the source of your fear in your immediate environment?

*) Is there an unfortunate event that can be a possible source of your anxiety?

*) Is there a meeting, event, or activity that might trigger your fear?

After due identification of the source of fear, you can easily apply the twenty-five practical tips presented in this book.

From the answers that you obtain, you can easily tell if your fears and worries are solvable. By knowing your fear, you can tell if you have enough faculties to deal with it accordingly. Remember, there are instances wherein only time can solve the problem and you can't do anything about it. If you think that the source of your anxiety is brought about your imagination, you need to do some serious effort to take it off your consciousness. If you think that the source of your fear is something real, then you need to take some solid steps to craft a plan of action. In crafting a plan, aside from getting aware of the 25 steps presented in this compendium, you need to answer the following questions:

*) What can be done to reduce the intensity of your worry or fear?

*) Can it be fixed within a short period of time or will you need some time?

*) In order to stop the problem from recurring, what can be done?

In the process, you need to think of the worst-case scenario. What's the worst that can happen? By doing so, you can be more critical and creative in coming up with solutions to your problems. Also, you can determine if you will need help from experts. You need to accept that things in life can be uncertain. By embracing uncertainty, you can stop worrying too much. This will help you become more open to a wide variety of solutions, hence the twenty-five practical tips presented in this book.

How To Simplify Your Life

In this twenty-first century, we seem to be losing control over our personal and professional lives. There seems to be not enough time to accomplish everything. Stress mounts daily, keeping up with the status quo becomes impossible, and life is just what you think it should be. This seemingly never-ending rat race has people yearning for a simpler, more meaningful way of life, and it is for these people that this book is written.

If you are looking for a *change* in your life, simplifying it can be the answer. "How to Simplify Your Life" is a simple process based on ten key ideas which each chapter presents. If you want an uncomplicated life, apply the principles that branch out from each key idea.

Additionally, this book provides many tips and techniques for simplifying specific areas in your life, from effective attitude change to simplified shopping. You can use these tips to work for you immediately. We've also included some time-honored principles that have served as good, solid advice for generations. This advice, along with the principles of simplifying your life, might seem deceptively simple. But they are powerfully effective when practiced consistently.

Whether you're intent on climbing the corporate ladder, whether you want to find a way to play more golf or make love more often, or whether you're deciding to raise a family, this book will help you find your focus, develop a plan, and simplify your life. Put these ideas to work and you'll find that you have the time and energy you need to make your life whatever you want it to be.

What It Means to Simplify Life

"Every cloud has a silver lining. Sometimes you just have to look for it."

– Anonymous

The alarm clock goes off; you pry your eyes open, swing yourself out of bed, and hit the floor running. You work your way—somewhat wildly—through the day, and before you know it, you are falling, exhausted, back into bed. Counting sheep is unnecessary. Instead you mumble, "There's gotta be a better way" three times before you drop off to sleep, dreaming about all the things you must accomplish tomorrow.

Whether you are the working person who deals with so much information everyday, the business owner who only has a business and no life, or the working mother whose time is divided for her kids and work, chances are, you are looking for a solution to your overextended lifestyle. If you are already convinced that there is a better way to get through each day, you are right. Simplifying your life might be the answer for you if you find yourself wishing for a better way of life for any of the following reasons:

You've had it with life in the fast lane. Life in the fast lane is wearing you out. Maybe you're just plain tired and can't seem to get rested. Life in the fast lane has lost its appeal and you want to get out.

You like the fast lane, but you'd like to go faster. You're firmly positioned on the fast track, and you're ready to go faster. The problem is, you can't seem to go any faster, because everyday life is littered with the obligatory clutter of life and you can't seem to find the time or the space you need to gather that extra speed you need to move ahead.

You're spending more time taking care of the stuff in your life than you are taking care of yourself. Your belongings are choking the progress of every single day, and you want to conquer the clutter once and for all, so that you can experience life free of the daily complications.

You're tired of jam-packed days where nothing seems to get done. Your action-packed days have you at the end of your rope. You don't have the energy, and you're tired of the anxiety.

Your relationships leave a lot to be desired. Your life is full of social obligations that you resent. On the other hand, your life might be dotted with people you care about, but you don't have any time for them.

You want each moment to count. You may have reevaluated your priorities and realized that there is more to life than work and other daily obligations and aggravations. Now is the time to make each moment count, and you just don't know how.

The person whose life is simplified does not generally have to worry about these issues. Such person who doesn't want to be in the fast lane is not there, and is doing fine. Such person who is on a fast track and looking to go faster is doing just that—efficiently and energetically.

Simplified life means the days are productive and clutter-free. It's knowing how to make each moment count so that ultimately you can get what you want out of life.

Simplifying Life Means Finding Time for Yourself

"Lives of great men all remind us we can make our lives sublime and, departing, leave behind us footprints in the sands of time."

– Henry Wadsworth Longfellow

Simplifying life promises to give you the time you need to do what you really want to do. But in order to get to that point, you might have to make some immediate changes in how you approach and use the time you already have.

How to Find More Time for Yourself

Budget and schedule your time. Treat your time as if it were a budget, and make sure that your budget includes time for yourself, at least every week, and every day if possible. Schedule that time on your calendar (whether it is thirty minutes or three hours) by making an appointment with yourself in writing. Treat that time as you would any confirmed appointment and resist the temptation to change it.

Prioritize. This is a vital step in simplifying life. You must learn to prioritize on a daily, as well as a long-term, basis. Not everything and everyone is equally important to your personal well-being, so keep this in mind as you schedule personal time for yourself. Remember, you are as important as anyone else, and time for yourself on a regular basis is going to give your life some much-needed balance.

Be selective. Spend less time on unimportant social obligations and concentrate on people who really matter to you. You'll probably find yourself with some spare time that you can then spend.

Learn to say no. You might be one of those people who say "yes" too often to requests for time from friends, family, and associates, only to wind up with no time for yourself. Say "yes" only if you have time or it is imperative that you become personally involved in the activity. And unless it is an emergency, don't change that appointment with yourself.

Have some quiet time. Ask others (such as family members) to respect your quiet time, and thank them often for their respect and acknowledgment. For example, insist on twenty minutes of personal quiet time when you get home from work and before you tackle domestic chores. It can make all the difference in how you feel and how you react to those around you.

Reduce your standards. It takes an inordinate amount of time to do things perfectly, and while you are busy being perfect, you are robbing yourself of time to do what you want to do. Compromise with yourself and relax your standards on how you do things, from work around the house to special projects.

Delegate. Stop doing everything yourself, and you'll have more time for yourself. Send out laundry, hire a gardener or a house cleaner, or have someone help you with your paperwork and filing. It doesn't cost as much as you think, and you'll be buying the best gift of all—the gift of time.

Consolidate. Keep a list of errands and try to do those in the same area all at once so you aren't driving all over town or making several trips. If you plan to cook a meatloaf, cook another one at the same time and freeze it.

Do away with daily time-wasters. Stop wasting time in bed in the morning. Spend less time in watching TV and using the social networking sites. Don't read junk mail. Don't feel obligated to finish an article you have started reading if it turns out to be boring or irrelevant.

Know the value of your time. Understand that every moment of your life, once spent, is gone forever.

330

With that in mind, plan to make every moment count.

Simplifying Life Begins with Adjusting Your Attitude

"The difference between the possible and the impossible lies in your determination."

– Tommy Lasorda

Attitude adjustment is an ongoing process that is directly related to growth. The attitude with which we embark on any new endeavor sets the tone and contributes mightily to the success or failure of that undertaking. Simplifying, as with so much in life, begins with attitude. A bad attitude will sabotage any success you might otherwise enjoy with a simplified life.

Committing to Change

Simplifying will require some action on your part, and some changes in the way you live. Change is inevitable. Resisting change puts an extra burden on your daily output, since it usually takes more time and effort than accepting it. Begin with your attitude toward change.

Always expect the unexpected. But make plans anyway; just factor in some flexibility in scheduling. Things don't always work out the way you'd like, and you need a little extra spur-of-the-moment time to deal with those disasters. On the other hand, opportunities knock when you least expect them, and some flexibility in your thinking and scheduling will let you take advantage of those delights that pop up from time to change.

Anticipate change. Then, when appropriate, don't fight it, embrace it. Things and people change. Jobs come and go, and people change and move in and out of your life, and a myriad of other changes are likely to be imposed upon you, whether you like it or not. Change often represents an opportunity to move on to a new, possibly more exciting, period in your life. Think about that when faced with change, and then act accordingly.

Becoming Less of a Procrastinator

Because simplifying is synonymous with getting things done, procrastination is one mental hurdle that absolutely must be mastered in order to get on the business of simplifying your life. Here are some tips to help you get out of the habit.

Stop dreaming up excuses—many people cannot be fooled.

Doing something is almost always better than doing nothing at all.

Force your way out of procrastination with critical do-or-die deadlines.

Make sure your working environment is pleasant, and that it suits you; also make sure you have needed supplies close at hand.

Tell a friend or colleague that you have to finish a project by a certain date, and check in regularly to report your progress.

Do the worst first; don't take the easy way out.

Tackle large projects by working on them in manageable segments.

Reward yourself regularly for competing all, or part, or a particularly odious task.

Adjusting your attitude really just means getting into the proper state of mind. Once you've done that, you'll be ready to prioritize and plan your simple living.

Prioritizing and Planning Things to Do

"The heavens themselves, the planets, and this center,
observe degree, priority and place."

– William Shakespeare

Projects seem to be an ongoing part of life; you no sooner finish one than you are faced with another. Worse, you can't seem to get one finished before the next begins, and you find yourself facing several projects that need your personal attention. It's unlikely that you will be able to eliminate projects from your life. But you can prioritize and manage the projects you do have, so that your life continues to be as simple as you want it to be, even with those projects.

Don't bite off more than you can chew. Stop agreeing to take on every project that comes down the pike. Take on only what you can comfortably assimilate into your simplified life. Learn to assess the payback value that goes with projects. If completing a project doesn't contribute to your life, either financially or emotionally, it's not worth taking on in the first place.

Focus your energies on one thing at a time. If you find yourself continuously stressed out by the many demands of multiple projects, perhaps you need to stop and take on only one project at a time.

Make yourself unavailable. If you have trouble getting projects done, make yourself unavailable to others when you are trying to get important work done. Lock yourself in your office and refuse to see anyone, and let your answering machine pick up your calls, or go to a place that has no distractions (such as a cabin in the woods that offers nice scenery, but no people, and no phones).

Change the way you do it. Don't do things one way just because they've always been done that way. Change how you handle projects so that you can get them done in a simplified manner. You can use a computer if it is faster, for example, even if it has always been done by hand.

Take the time to do it right the first time. You would save the time you would have otherwise spent redoing a poor job, and it will still be done.

Don't be obsessed by details. Don't get caught up in, or sidetracked by, details. Tackle the major components of any projects first; fine-tune the details later, if you have time.

Finish what you start. And don't start what you can't finish. Apply this thinking to the projects you consider taking on, and you can eliminate a lot of "undone project" agony before it has a chance to develop. The next time someone asks you to take on a project—even one you think, for some reason, you should—if you know deep down that it is one project to many, just say no!

Start the night before. Prepare your list for tomorrow, tonight.

Be realistic. Don't underestimate the amount of time it will take to complete a project or task. Be realistic, not fantastic.

Allocate your time. Include time for work, play, family, and spiritual matters, as well as regular time for yourself.

Use an appointment book. Get a good appointment book that you feel comfortable with, and make it an integral part of your daily life.

Keep it handy. Keep a calendar or appointment book near a telephone. If you tend to make appointments when you are out, carry one with you as well. You may also go digital—try Evernote on your computer or smartphone.

Review your accomplishments. At the end of the day, mark off the things you have done (from your to-do list and calendar), and carry over what still needs to be done, if necessary, onto another day on your schedule.

The most important thing in the process of simplifying your life is prioritizing and planning. Remember, only you can take control of your life rather than letting life control you.

Prioritizing the People in Your Life

"If you want to make good use of your time, you've got to know what's important and give it all you've got."

– Lee Laccoca

Unless you are a hermit or so obnoxious that no one can stand talking to you, you will deal with people on a regular basis. How you select which relationships to cultivate, and how you handle those relationships that are obligatory, can be directly affected by your prioritizing skills. These techniques below should help you prioritize when dealing with others.

Be realistic. Set realistic expectations for yourself and others. You'll make life a lot easier on yourself. Expecting people to do things for you—whether it's a family member, a friend, or a co-worker—can sometimes be unrealistic. When someone does help you out, consider it one of life's little bonuses.

Clarity check. Clarify your priorities and those priorities that others set for you (such as your boss). Be prepared to reset or revise those priorities from time to time as conditions in your life change unexpectedly.

Learn to say no. Say it pleasantly but firmly; never defensively. You cannot, nor should you have to, constantly accommodate everyone else's needs at the eventual expense of your own. Avoid adding an excuse, such as "I'm busy" to your no. People who aren't used to hearing you say no will only argue that their need takes priority. A simple, "No, I don't think so," or "No, but thanks for giving me the opportunity to help you," should get your point across.

Not everyone is equal. Everyone does not hold equal importance in your life. Some people are more important to you than others. Decide who has priority, and either eliminate spending time with those who don't have meaning, or cut down the time you spend with them so you can spend your time where it counts.

Balancing people and priorities. Friendships and relationships should be selected with great care. When they are treated with consideration and respect, they can last a lifetime. And a lifetime might not be long enough if time is used up with inconsequential people. If you find yourself neglecting people who matter to you because you don't have the time, perhaps you need to reevaluate your priorities so that you can put a little more balance in your life. You might have to force yourself to take the time to meet those special people; one sure-fire way is to buy tickets to events for yourself and your friends well in advance and book it on your schedule, as you would any other appointment.

If you can't find time to be with the family, try thinking of it this way: one of life's highest priorities is parenthood. With this in mind, housework, yard work, and yes, even the football game, should probably take a backseat to the most import duty of all—being a loving member of a family.

You can put your prioritizing skills to work by taking the time to reevaluate the relationships in your life so that you can allocate your time more justifiably—to spend with the people you really care about.

Eliminating Clutter

"Disposal is the handmaiden of an orderly mind."

– Norm Crampton

Now is the time to strip your life of nonessential things and affirm that you will resist the temptation to gather up a new hoard of possessions.

You can eliminate some excess baggage in your life by weeding out your possessions. If you're just storing it or worrying about it, it's time to get serious about eliminating it. Try the following elimination tips and techniques.

Eliminate needless duplication. Don't keep duplicate appliances, utensils, cosmetics and office supplies that you don't need. Generally speaking, you can use only one thing at a time.

Make elimination easy. Keep a large carton marked "elimination". Then, as you come across things you no longer need or use, put them in the box. Make sure the things in the box are given away at least once each month.

Give things away. Right away. Don't let anyone— including yourself—retrieve what has already been tossed or marked for giveaway. Get rid of things immediately, before anyone has time to consider.

Throw things away. Broken, rusty, bug-infested, mildewed, torn, or just plain useless items should be tossed without hesitation or remorse into the trash can.

Get it fixed. If you have something that is broken, or needs mending, get it fixed so it can be used or worn. Do this now.

Turn your trash into cash. If you are getting rid of things that have some value, you can either have a garage sale, or you can see if your local resale shop will take the items to sell for you. Just be reasonable about your financial expectations. Instead, be happy to have people pay you to haul away the stuff you don't want.

Set limits for your kids. Teach your children the elimination habit by example. If they're into the hoarding habit, insist on regular elimination sessions, with trips to a charity to get rid of the unwanted or outgrown items.

Share your books. A book, once read, serves no purpose if it just sits on a shelf for decoration. Keeping hundreds of books that you never look at is not impressive, contrary to what you might secretly think. More impressive is the act of passing books on for others to read. You can give your books to libraries, secondhand bookstores, and orphanages.

Rent rather than own. You can get rid of cumbersome equipment by renting things you seldom use. For example, if you ski only occasionally, you can rent the equipment.

Don't hang on to all your children's baby things forever. Someone needs them more than you do.

Eliminate car clutter. Keep a small trash can in the garage to use when you clean out the car. Then clean out the car every few days so the clutter won't get out of control.

Photo-mania. Cull through your photographs and get rid of duplicates, photos of people you don't recognize and poor quality or stupid shots.

Don't keep keys. Get rid of mysterious keys that you don't use because you have no idea what they unlock.

Take the disaster test. If an earthquake, fire, flood, or other natural disaster were to strike your life tomorrow, could you get by without gourmet gadgets, rarely used sports equipment, old trophies and plaques, old cosmetics, magazines and newspapers, and old college papers?

Belongings accumulate with no regard to your ever-changing perspective and overall needs. Often

those belongings do nothing but clutter up your life. Eliminate the clutter in your life by getting rid of the things that you do not need or use.

Simplifying Your Shopping

"That which you cannot give away, you do not possess. It possesses you."

— Ivern Ball

Shopping is one task that has to be done on a regular basis. Since shopping can't be eliminated altogether; no matter what you do, you'll still have to go to the grocery store regularly and make periodic forays out to shops and department stores for gifts, school clothes and supplies for children, new clothes for work or special occasion, and household goods.

Shopping Don'ts

Don't buy anything unless you have a place to put it. You'll just wind up with more clutter getting in the way of your simplified life.

Don't buy things just because they are on sale. If you don't really need something, buying it just because it is on sale is silly.

Don't buy clothes that don't go with anything. Don't get a fabulous skirt if you don't have at least a couple of tops to wear with it. You'll cram it into your closet and never wear it.

Don't buy shoes that hurt your feet. Life is too short to spend it breaking in shoes that do not stretch.

Shopping Do's

Keep a list. Keep a grocery list in the kitchen, and note items you need before you run out. This way, you'll always be fully stocked, and you won't have to waste time running to the store at the last minute. Use lists for other shopping needs as well, from gifts to clothes. Then, when you shop, shop with the list. If it's not on the list, don't buy it!

Take advantage of off hours, if you can. Whether at restaurants, department stores, or the post office, if you come during off hours you'll spend less time waiting in line, and receive better service. Avoid shopping when everyone else does (noontime, after work and weekends) if at all possible, and you'll save yourself lots of shopping aggravation along with the time.

Be strategic. When you have a day of shopping planned at the mall, start the day by parking your car at the opposite end of where you want to begin shopping. Walk to the other end to start shopping, and walk your way back toward the end of the mall where the car is parked.

Remember that everything you buy takes up space and requires care; it will need to be organized, stored, washed, dried, ironed, polished, and from time to time, maybe even repaired or mended. Don't buy things you don't need. Period.

Organizing Papers and Possessions

"Organizing is what you do before you do something, so that when you do it, it's not all mixed up."

– Christopher Robin in Winnie the Pooh

Getting and staying organized is a daily duty of a simplified life. When things are organized, your access to them, and the efficiency with which you can operate in relation to them, is minimized. Without attention to organization, simple living is impossible.

Organizing Papers

My contacts list. Keep all the business cards and phone numbers that you accumulate on scraps of paper in one place. Then, on a regular basis, transfer them to your computerized mailing list.

The owner's manual. Keep instructions near equipment. For example, keep the manual for the answering machine underneath it.

My organized office. If you handle paperwork at home, make sure you have an established work area assigned solely for doing and storing paperwork.

Clean your desk. Remember that the top of your desk is a work area, not a storage area. Therefore, get rid of things that are just being stored there, and only have papers that you are actually working on, or about to work on.

Go paperless note-taking. Install Evernote, or another note-taking software, on your computer and smartphone, and use it.

Organize as you go. Organize your paid bills as you go; don't just stuff hundreds of invoices and receipts into a box or large envelop.

Set up a simple filing system. And don't let your filing pile up. Set aside 10 to 15 minutes each day to keep on top of this vital organizational chore.

Back to Binders. Use three-hole binders to store and transport papers. Binders are particularly good for committee reports and minutes, and also can be used for financial records and address lists.

Check the children's papers. Don't wait until everyone is racing out the door in the morning to sign field trip permission slips or absence explanations.

Set limits. Limit yourself to a certain amount of space. If your filing cabinet gets full, don't buy another one; clean out the one you have and organize what's in it.

Organizing Possessions

A place for everything. Establish a place for everything, and then keep everything in its place. (How many times do you have to hear this?)

Convenience counts. Make your physical environment at work or at home convenient by having frequently used items readily accessible.

Container storage. Use your imagination along with some creative containers to organize categories of items that you can't live without.

Divide your drawers. Use dividers to keep your drawers organized, from your sock drawer to your bathroom drawers.

Hidden storage. Don't forget that you can store things in hidden areas, such as under the bed and behind couch.

Getting organized is a major commitment that produces bountiful benefits on a daily basis. What are you waiting for?

Managing Your Papers

"If you experience stress, you're doing it wrong."

– Jay Conrad Levinson

Papers need to be processed—either by filing them, or acting upon them, or by moving them to another point (hopefully out of your life). This daily demands means that you must be willing to establish and maintain all the systems required to process, move, and store your papers.

Papers on the go. Set up files in your briefcase marked "to do," "to pay," "to file," and "to read," so you can keep your papers organized on the go.

Get ready to read. Keep a pair of scissors and a stapler in your "to read" basket. That way you can clip articles and throw the rest of the magazine away before it ever has a chance to hit the basket.

Use project carts. Make use of rolling file carts for the projects. Set up temporary files for the project, organized appropriately.

Ready, set, go. Establish a "to-go" area for papers, outgoing mail, and files that you need to take with you when you leave. This area is preferably close to the door so you won't forget to check it when you leave.

Keep a master file for emergencies. Make sure you keep a master file that someone close to you knows about. Include pertinent information that will be needed in case something happens to you, such as the location of your will, ownership documents and bank records, credit card numbers, and insurance policies.

Use a simple alphabetical system. When setting up your files, resist the urge to color-code, index, or otherwise turn what should be simple paper storage system into a convoluted nightmare that takes extra time to set up and maintain.

Don't let the filing pile up on you. See to it that you file papers into your system on a regular basis. A filing system is useless if you ignore it and pile instead of file.

Check with the CPA, the IRS, and the law. Check with your attorney, your CPA, or the IRS to find out how long you need to keep records; date them with an expiration date before they go into storage; and each year toss the files that have reached the expiration date.

Conquering the paper pile-up by systematizing is crucial to simple living; without systems, chaos reigns.

Systematizing Your Home

"With my invitations I send directions as a guide, but my house is such as mess that they need a map for the inside."
– Phyllis Diller

Assuming that—regardless of your best efforts of elimination—you still have a substantial inventory of belongings, you will need a system for maintaining those things in a streamlined, effective manner. Unfortunately, there are no magic systems for simple daily maintenance. Here are a few simple ideas on how to take care of yourself and your belongings.

Keep things near their area of use. For example, pans need to be kept near the stove, and the *TV Guide* should always be kept near the television. Then put things back where they belong. And insist everyone in the house to do the same.

Everybody pitches in. If you are a member of a family, insist that each member who is old enough assume responsibility for at least some of their personal maintenance.

Write it down. Don't automatically pick up after children and spouses. Write down chores and other obligations so they can't say they didn't know, or forgot what they were supposed to do. Then post the chore list for everybody to see.

Use support services. One of the best methods for hanging daily maintenance—from doing laundry and housework to running errands—is to hire someone else to do it for you. You can drop your clothes off at a commercial laundry, you can get a housekeeper to come in once a week to clean, and you can use an errand service to do your errands—from trips to the grocery store to taking the cat to the vet.

Take things with you. Consolidate trips. If you have to go down to the basement to get something, take whatever needs to be returned with when you go. Designate a spot at the top and bottom of stairs to collect items going up or down the stairs to be put away.

Daily duty. Spend at least a few minutes each day in each room of the house at least picking up and putting away any clutter that may have accumulated.

Tidy up the night before. Each evening, take a few minutes to straighten things up and get your clothes ready for the following day. This way, you won't have to get up to yesterday's mess.

Clean before you sit. Clean off the counters and put pots and pans in the sink to soak before you sit down and eat.

Brush, soak, clean. Since 75 percent of cleaning is chemical, don't spend so much time and energy scrubbing things. Brush off loose dirt, then soak the item, then clean.

Do it in the nude. Try doing the housework naked. Involve your spouse, if you like. It's a new way of doing things that might just put a little joy and amusement into what would otherwise be just an obnoxious chore.

Simple Tips for Your Closet

Complementary arrangement. Put blouses or shirts with complementary skirts or pants. Those things that don't go with anything in your closet should be set aside to be given away.

Categorize. Hang all your clothes on categories: skirts, pants, blouses, shirts, jackets, suits, dressy clothes, etc. Then mix and match at will.

Total look. You can hang complete outfits together, such as a blouse, skirt, and jacket, so that you don't have to rack your brain trying to remember what goes with what, and you can grab an entire ensemble and dress quickly.

Color palette. However you group your clothes, you'll want to keep them organized within the groups by color. This helps you coordinate your clothes that much quicker.

You can design your own systems for maintaining your daily life. Systems apply to everything from housework to career planning and managing your leisure time. Be creative and keep it simple, but keep it systematized.

How to Apply Key Ideas for the Best Results?

It is all too easy to fall off the "simple life" wagon. Getting sidetracked by life's daily details and demands can mean that your attitude slips, you forget to prioritize, somehow you start accumulating more than you need—and fall into the chasm of disorganization, with any systems you had in place, gradually disintegrating as the final coup de grâce.

The best way to combat this possibility is to remind yourself every day why you want, and need, a simple life—what it really means to you. With your reason firmly fixed in your mind, quickly review the ten key ideas for simplifying life, and commit yourself to applying at least two of the principles each day.

Remember this: *If you are willing, you can make it happen.*

Whatever you do and however you do it, do it daily. Be persistent. Your life can be as simple as you are willing to let it be. It can stay as simple as you are committed to making it. It's entirely up to you.

How To Stop Being Insecure

Insecurity is an inevitable human feeling. Not being contented with oneself is part of human nature, but we can reduce the intensity of this discontentment. Insecurity may be difficult to avoid, but its effects are reducible. Uncontrolled insecurity may produce many different negative consequences for the individual, which is why it must be addressed at the earliest possible time.

The most basic test to know whether you are experiencing insecurity or not is to ask yourself the question—"Are there times when I think that I'm not good enough?" If your answer to this question is no, then you are safe from insecurity. But if your answer to this question is yes, then you are certainly feeling insecure about something. Low self-esteem is one of the clear symptoms of insecurity.

There are a lot more ways to determine whether you are experiencing insecurity or not, and this book shall tackle those different ways on a case-to-case basis.

This book is designed to help the individual overcome insecurity in order to achieve a fulfilled life. The absence of insecurity in oneself allows us to live our lives to the fullest and allows us to enjoy the different opportunities presented to us. On the other hand, the constant feeling of being insecure hinders us from developing our skills and making the most out of what is given to us.

So what are you waiting for?

If you wish to overcome your insecurities, then the first thing to do is to read the tips presented in this book one by one. At the end of the book, a summary shall be provided. The most important tip to be followed is: take action. Apply these tips to yourself and be prepared to face the world, insecurity-free!

Identify the Source of Your Insecurities

"Our problems are man-made, therefore they may be solved by man. And man can be as big as he wants. No problem of human destiny is beyond human beings."

— John F. Kennedy

The first step to overcome any problem in life is to identify its cause. You need to trace things backward in order to know how to move forward. This process also applies to defeating one's insecurities. Before trying to overcome something, you must start with knowing the source.

This step is crucial because it is from this step that all points of action shall take place. Once you have identified the source of your insecurities, you already know full well what you are up against. If you are still confused, some of the common sources of insecurity are: being surrounded by over-achievers, being underappreciated, being left out and rejected, being influenced by standards of society and having low self-esteem.

When you are surrounded by people who have their achievements hanging on their chests, there is a tendency for you to feel a certain pang of jealousy towards them. Don't worry; this is normal. However, how you act on this jealousy makes all the difference. Some people treat this jealousy as a motivation to work harder in order to achieve the same kind of success. On the other hand, there are people who treat this jealousy as a source of devastation because they feel like they can never attain the same kind of achievement. Insecurity develops when you are constantly surrounded by these types of people. When everyone around you is doing well on their own, people tend to compare you with them. Comparison often always leads a person to think what could be wrong with them, and it makes a person ask questions such as what do other people have that he/she does not have.

If you are constantly in the company of over-achievers and you are not doing anything about it, some people may underappreciate your skills and capabilities and might treat you as if you were invisible, but this is not a reason for you to be discouraged; most importantly, you should not think lowly of yourself just because other people do this. If there are people who should feel lowly of themselves, it is these people who bring you down. Don't let what other people tell you dictate how you live your life. As you will see later on, the skills of these "overachievers" are not the only skills in the world, and these should not be the only standards for appreciating someone.

Moreover, rejection is not the end of the world. Just because other people leave you out does not mean that you should allow yourself to be left out. Insecurity is often developed in people who are constantly left out because they are given the feeling that they are not wanted and that they cannot contribute anything substantial. As a way of fighting against your insecurities, you may use rejection as a means of improving yourself in order to avoid this kind of feeling in the future. Do not use it as a depressant! Show these people that they made a mistake in leaving you out.

One of the biggest causes of insecurity is when one is surrounded by societal norms/standards. The society where we belong to often has a notion of what is considered "good," "beautiful," "handsome," etc. However, they fail to acknowledge that these standards are highly flexible and can be bended at any time. Still, many people do not know about this flexibility and the result is feeling bad about themselves when they do not conform to these standards.

Lastly, low self-esteem branches from a combination of the abovementioned common causes of insecurity. When you do not have self-confidence and you do not believe in yourself, then you will always feel insecure about every little thing.

Now that we have provided some of the most common causes of insecurity, it is time for you to identify yours. Identify yours now in order to proceed to solving your problems!

Acknowledge Your Fears

"Don't be afraid of your fears. They're not there to scare you. They're there to let you know that something is worth it." – C. Joybell C.

After you have identified the source of your insecurities, then you are also on the way of identifying your fears. It is highly possible that the source of your insecurities also includes the source of your fears. For you to find out, you must be objective and a keen observer.

What exactly are you afraid of? Take time to think—list all the things that you are feeling insecure of, and list all the things that you are afraid of and how they contribute to your insecurity. Common examples are disappointment, rejection and not being good enough in the eyes of others. Acknowledge these fears; for when you acknowledge them, it means that it is clear to you what exactly they are, how they affect your life, and it makes you think about what you should do about them.

For example, you fear disappointment and rejection. Disappointment may come in different forms— disappointment from your parents, from your peers or even from yourself. But why must you fear disappointment? It is perfectly normal. People make mistakes all the time; everyone is capable of disappointment. When you fear disappointment, you take time to examine your every action to the point that you are already acting like a robot: very scripted and barely moving out of free will. Does this bring about positive effects in your life? No.

When you fear not being good enough in the eyes of others, then you are allowing your insecurities to take over your life. Who cares what other people say? As we shall discuss later on, societal norms are created by people too. These norms are not always good. They do provide some sort of order in this chaotic world, but when people become too engrossed in them, these norms become a source of problems because people already allow themselves to be controlled by them.

Face your fears. The only way to fight the enemy is to know the enemy.

Consider Your Strengths

"Nothing can dim the light which shines from within."

– Maya Angelou

As was mentioned before, people tend to develop insecurities when they think they are not good enough and that they don't have the necessary skills to feel good about themselves. This should not be the case. Every person has his/her own unique strengths, yet sometimes we take things for granted, including our strengths. However, no other person can identify your strengths more accurately than yourself. The most that other people can do for you is to guide you in the process of knowing what your strengths are, but the confirmation must come from you.

How do you identify your strong areas? There are plenty of ways to do it, but one way is to consider the things which make you feel the happiest and most fulfilled. What is that thing and/or activity that you want to do all the time? What is that thing that you are always craving for? What is that thing that gives you a feeling of contentment and self-fulfillment? What are the things that you can do without difficulty? Try answering these questions, and you will be able to identify your strong areas soon enough.

Take sports for example. Some people are considered good in sports, and they admit that sports are their strong area because they enjoy playing sports, they find sports a very relaxing and fulfilling activity, sports excite them and they can play sports without much difficulty. Try using these criteria in other areas for you to find out your strong areas.

Do not be afraid to consider your strengths. Stop telling yourself that you are not good enough. You may not be skilled in a certain area where a lot of people excel, but there is always an area that you have extraordinary skills on. If you are still unaware of what your strengths are, it will be helpful to explore a lot of possibilities in order to find out what these are. If you are already aware of your strengths yet you just find it hard to acknowledge them, it is time for you to stop this line of thinking.

If you really wish to build up your self-esteem and defeat your insecurities, you must start with considering your strengths.

Acknowledge Your Successes and Achievements

"Success is peace of mind which is a direct result of self-satisfaction in knowing you did your best to become the best you are capable of becoming."

– John Wooden

If ever you feel like you have never achieved anything in your life, you are wrong. Surely, there must be something that you have achieved in the past that you should be proud of. Instead of dwelling in your "failures" and in the times when you felt that you are not enough, why don't you try dwelling in your successful times? Try to remember what these successes are and make these your driving forces to overcome your insecurities.

These successes can come in different forms. If you think that the achievements you see in other people are the only achievements there are in this world, then you are wrong. You surely have accomplished something in your life; you are not paying much attention to it because you are degrading such achievements. Remember that every achievement is something to be proud of, no matter how big or small they are. Do not take them for granted.

What could these achievements be? Educational achievements are common ones. Extracurricular achievements are another. But achievements mean more than trophies on one's arms and medals around one's neck. You can say that you have also achieved something when you have helped others become better people—for example, a person is going through a really tough stage in his/her life, and you were able to give him/her reasonable advice that helped him/her afterwards. Another example is: you can say that you have achieved something when you have successfully uplifted someone's spirits. Let's say that your friend is having a bad day, but you kept him/her company, and at the end of the day, he/she told you that he/she is grateful that you were there and that you provided a source of comfort. These are also achievements, only intangible ones. But even if these are just little things, these are also things to be proud of; these show that you are not a useless person. You have worth in this world, and you should know by now that you must always see your worth even if other people do not because there will always be people who can say that you have achieved something worthwhile in your life.

Acknowledging your successes and achievements is also a helpful way of discovering your strengths. If you have achieved several things in a particular area, then there is a huge possibility that this area is your forte.

Ask Friends to Help You Identify Your Best Qualities

"Encourage, lift and strengthen one another. For the positive energy spread to one will be felt by us all. For we are connected, one and all."

– Deborah Day

It has been said before that only you can identify what exactly are your strengths—but your friends can also help you with it. Ask those who are closest to you to help you identify your best qualities. Choose the set of friends whom you know will be completely honest with you. Ask them to write down or to tell you the qualities about you that they like most.

Once you have gathered a list of your best qualities from the people you trust the most, keep this list with you and use it as a source of motivation. When things go wrong, simply go back to this list. When you feel like you've been a very bad person, look at this list, and you will see that you are not one. You will see that other people can see you for who you really are, and not just as a product of the standards of society. The best that you can do is to believe in what your friends listed down—because these are the qualities that they see as an observer. You can always deny that you possess these qualities, but remember that actions speak louder than words. You may deny that you are not this type of person, but your friends can attest to it that they see you as one with those beautiful qualities.

Furthermore, it is helpful to do this exercise because 1) it will help you identify your strengths better; 2) it will help boost your self-esteem because you will be reminded of the things that people like about you; and 3) you will have the chance to improve the skills which are not mentioned as your "best" ones.

Looking at this list of qualities, you can assess whether these are your strong qualities or not. It will help boost your self-esteem because it will remind you that you are not worthless. And most importantly, you will see from an observer's point of view the things you are good at, and you will be able to take it from there the areas or the qualities that you are not that good at. This should not be a source of insecurity but rather as a motivating force for improvement.

You already have the foundations of a secure character by virtue of those qualities, and you can always add more qualities to your "best" list by striving to improve yourself.

Surround Yourself with Supportive People

"Every person needs support from others to be able to reach his/her dreamland."

– Euginia Herlihy

One of the best ways to overcome insecurity is to be surrounded by people who support you in everything you do because insecurities are only made worse if you choose to surround yourself with people who bring you down.

Surround yourself with people who are not judgmental, those who are willing to help you accomplish your goal of overcoming your insecurities. These people can be your family, your friends, your significant other and most particularly those people who are undergoing the same kind of healing process. The last group of people is the most effective support group that one can have because in this state, you are surrounded by the people who know *exactly* what you are going through, and together, you can come up with solutions to your problems.

But this doesn't mean that your family, friends and/or partner do not count as significant. They are also very important sources of inspiration and strength because the road towards changing yourself and your perspectives is not an easy one. There will always be times when you will feel like giving up because changing one's mindset cannot be done in an instant—it requires a lot of hard work, but having a support group by your side can always ease the burden of your problems.

Another significant reason why a support group is important is that these people know you for who you are; they might possibly be the same people who helped you come up with your "best qualities" list. Thus, you know that these people will be honest to you no matter what. When something's wrong, they will not hesitate to tell; when things go right, they will uplift your spirit. It is important to be surrounded by these kinds of people because truthfulness to oneself and to others plays a very important role in overcoming your insecurities.

Never underestimate the power of a support group. They are always there for you, they will not judge you and they will be there to guide you along the way.

Avoid Being Around People Who Make You Feel Insecure

"There are many good seeds in you. Therefore you must avoid every bad soil in the world."

– Israelmore Ayivor

In relation to the previous tip, it is important to surround yourself with people who make you feel good about yourself and not those who intensify your insecurities. Even if the said people are the ones you've been around with for the longest time, if they cause you more bad feelings than the good ones, then it is time to let them go. Distance yourself from these people. When we have been surrounded by the same kind of people our whole lives and we have seen them achieve one thing after another, it could produce the feeling of being left behind and being incapable of achieving anything.

The only way to stop these insecurities from forming is to remove the source. Maybe the reason why you cannot stop feeling bad about yourself is because you are constantly surrounded by the people who push your confidence level down, make you feel unappreciated, reject you and insist on the standards imposed by society.

Why torture yourself? Why do you have to be surrounded by these people? You don't. Beyond pleasing others, beyond conforming to society's standards, you must think of yourself first. Save yourself from the emotional pain.

How can you avoid these people? Simple. Just try. If you are used to being with these people in your everyday workplace, then it's time for you to get to know other people. Look for reasons to avoid them—these need not be lies, but there are plenty of reasons available. Engross yourself in your tasks so that you don't have to pay attention to them. Sooner or later, you will see that you have successfully broken free from their company and that their opinions no longer matter to you.

If they are the reasons for the development of your insecurities, then it is just right for you to detach yourself from them in order to give yourself room to grow.

Socialize More

"Be genuinely interested in everyone you meet and everyone you meet will be genuinely interested in you."

– Rasheed Ogunlaru

It cannot be denied that we tend to overthink when we are alone because there is nothing to preoccupy our minds from wandering off to other sorts of thoughts. If you already have insecurity problems, then it is highly probable that you will often think of these problems when you are alone. When you spend too much time dwelling on your insecurities, they build up because you throw in one theory after another. As a solution to this problem, you must socialize with others more, and try meeting new friends in order to prevent having too much alone time with yourself.

Meeting somebody for the first time often makes people nervous. However, meeting new friends can actually be a good thing. New friends can make you discover your hidden strengths and skills because different people bring out different sides of us each time we get to know them, depending on your favorite topics of discussion. As the exchange of ideas goes on and on, you will see that your mind is no longer focused on your insecurities but rather on the new things that you have learned from your friends.

You must remember how important it is to have friends to support you when you are feeling down. Opening yourself to other people, socializing with them and building nurturing relationships can help you realize that you're not an awful person after all, contrary to what you first perceived yourself to be.

If you're not a very sociable person, that's not a problem at all. You simply have to try. When friends ask you out, join them. Who knows? Maybe you'll meet your greatest friend on that day. Some people are naturally shy and are hesitant to socialize with others, but once you meet people whom you get along with, you will realize that you shouldn't have been shy at all, and you will wish that you've known these people longer. In short, do not be afraid to meet new people. New people bring different surprises to our lives.

Lastly, remember that many friends are better than few when it comes to providing moral support in your hardest battles.

Identify What Hinders You from Overcoming Your Insecurities

"The best way to treat obstacles is to use them as stepping-stones. Laugh at them, tread on them, and let them lead you to something better."

– Enid Blyton

There are times when we are more than willing to do something, but then something is stopping us from executing our plans. The question is, what is this "something," and how can you get rid of it?

This applies also to overcoming your insecurities. Let us assume that you are already clear about what your insecurities are, what you are afraid of and that you are willing to defeat these insecurities; but then something is stopping you. Ask yourself: what is blocking your way?

It is difficult to take action when you have obstacles along your way, most especially when you have all the willpower and motivation, but something else does not want you to proceed. Still, remember that no journey comes without obstacles. A journey without obstacles often does not contain lessons for us to cherish. Identify what these obstacles are and make a move towards eliminating these in order for you to begin defeating your insecurities.

Even though there are hindrances to your desired goals, do not be discouraged. Remember that these hindrances are temporary, and they are called "obstacles" because they are meant to be surpassed. Establish that willpower to defeat your insecurities and maintain this said willpower in surpassing the obstacles along your way, and surely, nothing can stop you from living a life full of fulfillment.

Another way to motivate yourself is to think of these obstacles as blessings in disguise. They may block your way and make your journey difficult, but they will surely make your journey worth it. They may be the source of headaches, disappointment and doubt, but the end-product of surpassing these obstacles is always a nice thing to aim for.

Do not be discouraged. Will yourself to overcome these obstacles, and you will find yourself one step further in overcoming your insecurities.

Always Make a Reality Check

"Reality is that which, when you stop believing in it, doesn't go away."

– Philip K. Dick

Sometimes, insecurities are developed due to our paranoia about the things happening around us. Since this is the source of the problem, then the solution is to learn the art of separating imagination from reality.

This kind of insecurity usually occurs in relationships. When you are in a relationship with someone and you feel insecure, you usually think that you are not good enough for your partner and/or your partner might find someone else because you do not satisfy his/her standards. Oftentimes, these kinds of insecurities root from rumors and/or paranoia.

In this type of situation, the best thing for you to do is to get your facts straight first before reacting to anything. When one does not have confidence in himself/herself, he/she has a hard time debunking rumors and believing truths. This should not be the case. Be as objective as you can and try to understand the situation from an impartial point of view.

Consider this example: two people in a relationship often fight because the woman often assumes that the man is up to something because "she can see it in his actions," such as picking up the phone late; but she does not have concrete proof. She is insecure about their relationship, so she claims that she can "see it falling apart," but what's wrong in this picture? She does not have any proof to back up her claim. All of her accusations are rooted from her interpretations of the man's actions. What's with picking up the phone late? Does this automatically mean that the relationship is falling apart? No. But this kind of thinking *will* lead to a strained relationship if it is continued.

In this kind of situation, the person has failed to make a reality check because she is too caught up with her imaginary scenarios. The best way to go around this problem is to stop trying to read minds. Stop trying to put meaning in every action without factual basis, for this will only cloud your judgment and will cause strains in your relationship with other people.

Moreover, do not allow your insecurities to cloud your judgment. Do not let your insecurities take reality away from you; do not let insecurities make you lose connection with the truth.

Stop Comparing Yourself to Others

"Comparison is the death of joy."

– Mark Twain

One of the most common sources of insecurity is comparison to others. There are plenty of times when this cannot be avoided, most especially if there are stark, obvious differences between you and the other person. Although there are times when this is unavoidable, you must still do your best to avoid doing such.

Comparison to others often happens when you see things and/or characteristics in another person that you do not see in yourself. But the question to ask is how sure are you that you do not possess these characteristics as well? This is one of the dangers of comparison—it prohibits you from realizing your full potential because you are already setting up boundaries to yourself as the opposite of another person.

Comparison also occurs when another person has certain skills that you do not, particularly when these skills are your "frustrated" skills. Another question to ask is how sure are you that you are incapable of these skills? What if you only *think* you are incapable of excelling in these certain areas, but actually, you have the potential to be skilled in this area?

Comparison also brings dangers when they are done with other people. You cannot control what other people will say about you; the only thing you can control is how you will react to these opinions. Do not mind the comparisons that they make—you know what you are capable of, and you know what your possible skills are. Do not be blinded by the comparisons that they make; they are only looking at you from a second-person point of view. It is you, the individual, who matters.

Remember that every person is unique.

Do Not Make Your Insecurities Obvious

"Don't let fear or insecurity stop you from trying new things. Believe in yourself. Do what you love. And most importantly, be kind to others, even if you don't like them."
– Stacy London

It is a given fact that you are feeling insecure about certain things, but this doesn't mean that you have to let it show. Doing so would only give you an image of vulnerability. Show people that you are not affected, for whatever they may say about you may add to your burden of defeating your insecurities.

Do not let other people see that you are weak. Project yourself as a strong individual, even when you're still at the point that you're trying to defeat your insecurities. Doing so would not only help you by preventing other people from perceiving you as weak, but doing so would also train you to become confident around other people.

In relation to the tip to stop reading minds, you must not assume that other people can see that you have insecurities. Knowing, or simply thinking, that other people can see your weak side will only make you more conscious and will make your actions more limited. If you do the opposite thing, however, no one will have to notice the problems that you are going through.

Showing your insecurities to other people would only make them get worse; it is better if you keep them to yourself and show only to the people whom you trust.

Discuss Your Feelings

"If you have the words, there's always a chance that you'll find the way."

– Seamus Heaney

Another basic way to overcome your insecurities is to let it all out. Discuss your feelings with someone else, particularly your best friend or someone who you know will understand you completely. Letting it all out is a way of acknowledging it, and when you acknowledge it, you know what you are fighting against.

There is something very comforting about being able to express your feelings completely. Keeping all these feelings and emotions locked up inside you is difficult and causes you a lot of pain and anxiety. On the other hand, letting these be known by the people you trust gives you a feeling of security and comfort. Remember that these people whom you trust will not judge you for how you feel, but instead they are there to make you feel better.

Discussing your feelings with other people is not only beneficial to you as you will be given advice by other people, but it is also beneficial to others because they will learn from your experiences.

If you find it hard to discuss your feelings with other people, do yourself a favor by at least looking for a medium to be able to express your feelings. Do you often find yourself lost when it comes to the spoken word? Maybe you'll express yourself better in terms of the written word. Try blogging or keeping a journal where you can record your thoughts. This way, you don't have to let the tension build up inside you. Moreover, keeping a record of your thoughts is also important when it comes to tracking down your progress of recovery. At first it may seem like all of your journal entries are full of doubt and insecurities, but as you go on, you will see the changing trend in your entries, and by then, you can see that you are making progress towards overcoming your insecurities.

Discussing your feelings does not only make the burden a little lighter, but it also allows you to receive advice from other people.

Remember That You Create Your Own Destiny

"The only person you are destined to become is the person you decide to be."

– Ralph Waldo Emerson

Similar to the thought that you must not compare yourself with others, remember that you create your own destiny. Remember that you are a unique individual and that you will always be capable to do things as long as you will it.

Do not be affected by what other people say about you. It is our choices, not other people's, that determine what happens in our lives and how we will live our lives.

Keeping in mind that you create your own destiny will help you disregard whatever degrading or underestimating statements people say. In addition to that, keeping in mind that you are in control of your own life is a good start towards defeating your insecurities. You must know that you are the one who decides what is best for you, and you are the one who knows exactly what you want and what you are afraid of.

Live your life the way you want to live it, not according to what society dictates. Yes, there are certain rules that must be followed, but in terms of skills and character development, you must not be limited to the labels society gives people. As such, one of the main reasons why you feel insecure is because you are not in control of your own life, and you allow other people's opinions to influence you completely.

Instead of conforming to everything that society says, break away if you must. Do your own thing. Do not be afraid; you might be even starting a new trend. You are free to do whatever you want as long as it is legal. In terms of your development, lead your life in such a way that you will attain happiness and self-fulfillment in the end.

Remember that there is no other person who should run your life but *you*.

Take Risks to Change Your Behavior

"If you dare nothing, then when the day is over, nothing is all you will have gained."

– Neil Gaiman

No matter how difficult it is to face your fears, remember that it will all be worth it in the end. Take risks to change your behavior if you really wish to completely defeat your insecurities. There will be plenty of challenges in the way, but you must believe that you are capable of overcoming these challenges.

For you to be more convinced to take risks, try weighing the short-term and long-term effects of your actions. As a rational being, through your evaluation, you know which will produce the most positive consequences, and you know which will produce the effects that will benefit you better and longer.

On the one hand, thinking short-term would only lead you to think that risking a lot of things for the sake of defeating your insecurities is a waste of time. Because overcoming one's insecurities is a tiresome task, it takes a lot of courage and risk to succeed. Some people think that they should not bother addressing their insecurities because they are already "happy" and they are "already living the life that they want," but is this the life that they want to live for the rest of their lives? Will this short-term thinking benefit them? Only thinking of the immediate effects will not reap the best benefits.

Going to the other side of the coin, thinking of the long-term effects of your decision to defeat your insecurities will make you realize that there are a lot of sacrifices, choices and hard decisions to be made. However, think about it:

living with your insecurities may be fine today, but will it still be fine tomorrow? If you think long-term, you will see that all the risk will be worth it given the positive effects of overcoming your insecurities—such as self-fulfillment, character and skills development, etc.

Just because a task is difficult does not mean that it is not worth undertaking. Sometimes, it is in these arduous tasks where we learn the greatest life lessons; and it is in these tasks where we not only improve ourselves once we have attained the end goal, but we improve ourselves even *during* the process of doing these tasks itself.

There is nothing wrong with taking risks even though the end is still unclear. Keep in mind that the lessons and the experiences along the way are ones that you will keep forever.

Develop Courage within Yourself

"Courage is the most important of all the virtues because without courage, you can't practice any other virtue consistently."

— Maya Angelou

Alongside taking risks, you must develop enough courage to do so. The battle towards defeating your insecurities is not an easy one, which is why you have to be strong in the process.

Following Maya Angelou's quote, you cannot proceed without courage. You cannot proceed to doing any of the tips provided in this book if you do not have the courage and the willpower to do so.

A way of developing courage within yourself is to weigh the pros and cons of what you are about to do. As you can see, defeating insecurities has more pros than cons, for they possess long-term effects, and achieving this goal will change your life forever. This should be enough to motivate a person to go for it.

Sometimes, the best things in life are not meant to be achieved easily. They have to be gained through hard work. This is where courage comes in. Develop courage within yourself, and you will succeed in anything you wish.

Consider the Negative Consequences of Insecurity

"Try giving up all the thoughts that make you feel bad, or even just some of them, and see how doing that changes your life. You don't need negative thoughts. All they have ever given you was a false self that suffers. They are all lies."

– Gina Lake

One of your greatest motivations to finally start defeating insecurity is to think of the negative consequences that it entails. How is insecurity affecting your life? Surely it is not affecting your life in a good way. Wouldn't you want to change something that does not affect your life in a positive manner? A list of the negative consequences of insecurity would serve as a guide.

If you know that something is not bringing about positive effects in your life, wouldn't you want to get rid of this thing? This is exactly the same for insecurity. You must know that insecurity does not do you any good. In fact, it causes the entire opposite—you feel bad about yourself, you do not have confidence, your personal growth is stinted, you cannot maximize your potentials, and you feel afraid to try new things. Seeing that these are the negative effects of insecurity, isn't it enough of a wake-up call to you that you need to change?

A way to remind yourself of these negative consequences is to imagine yourself in the worst situations possible. As you imagine yourself, think about it; would you want to live your life this way? Would you be happy living in fear, always in doubt and never sure of anything? These are just sample, imagined scenarios that you can think of; there are plenty of others, but this is just a way of illustrating how important it is to weigh in the positive and negative consequences of one's actions.

Remember that insecurity will not do you any good, thus you must work towards removing this negativity in your life. Not doing so might lead these worst imagined scenarios become a reality.

Think of the Positive Effects of Overcoming Insecurity

"A positive attitude may not solve all your problems, but its effect will make it worth the effort."

– Jeffrey Fry

In relation to listing down the negative effects of insecurity in your life, it is also important to weigh in the positive consequences. If the negative effects can serve as your motivating force to defeat insecurity, then the same goes with the positive effects. In the process of trying to overcome insecurity, it will get very difficult, but you must hold on. When you are in doubt or when you feel like you cannot go on further, just think of the rewards waiting for you at the end of the whole process. The whole process is a tough one, but you must be assured that it will be worth it.

What are the possible positive effects of overcoming insecurity? Heightened self-esteem, better socialization with others, character and personal development are among the many positive results of overcoming insecurities.

You must always keep your focus on the positive side of things and not on the negative. Do not dwell too much on the negative, for they are meant to bring you down. Focus on the positive and allow this positivity to be reflected in your personality, and you will see the difference that it makes.

Focusing on the positive does not only include thinking of the positive effects of your actions, it also means always looking at the bright side of things. When faced with a difficult situation, what do you do? A pessimist will simply give up and think that his efforts have gone to waste while an optimist will see this difficult situation as an opportunity for personal development and simply as another challenge that is highly possible to overcome.

It is always better to stay on the positive side of things rather than the negative. Staying positive amidst everything will cost you no harm while being negative will just bring you further down.

Think of these positive effects, and imagine how good your life would be once you start to enjoy these effects, and surely you will be more motivated to fight against insecurity.

Always Be True

" When we turn around & come face to face with our destiny, we discover that words (spoken) are not enough. I know so many people who are brilliant speakers but are quite incapable of practising what they preach. It's one thing to describe a situation & quite another to experience it. I realised a long time ago that a warrior in search of his dream must take his inspiration from what he actually does & not from what he imagines himself doing."

– Paulo Coelho

Yes, you are trying to change yourself. And yes, you want to get rid of your insecurities. Despite these noble intentions, you must remember that it is necessary to stay true to yourself at all times. In the process of trying to overcome our sense of worthlessness and/or lack of self-esteem, we tend to try changing our personalities into another personality that is very different from who we really are. We end up being pretentious, trying to live a life that is far from reality, one which we know will make other people regard us highly.

There is no good in this kind of practice. It is a given fact that you are working your way towards overcoming your insecurities. That's a good start. But it should be done in an honest manner. If you are trying to change yourself, then you must change yourself into a person that is fundamentally who you are, not someone whose personality has been influenced by societal norms.

What makes us pretend? Societal norms. It cannot be emphasized further that one of the reasons why people become insecure is because sometimes they feel like they do not conform to the "norms" or standards of beauty, intelligence, etc. What people forget is that these norms are only created by people and that these do not dictate what is absolutely right and what is absolutely wrong, in the same way that these norms do not give us a complete picture of what is absolutely beautiful or not. For these reasons, we must not fear going against these norms.

We must break free from the chains of these norms for us to live an honest and fulfilling life.

Learn to Let Go of the Things That Make You Insecure

"You will find that it is necessary to let things go; simply for the reason that they are heavy. So let them go, let go of them. I tie no weights to my ankles."

– C. Joybell C.

We have been talking about removing the cause of the problem for quite a while, but this point needs to be emphasized again and again so as it is not forgotten. In order to move on with your life, insecurity-free, you must learn to let go of the things that give you these insecurities. There is a possibility that these things are very dear to you, particularly if these are people who are special to you yet make you feel bad, but just think of the effect that they have on you.

Nothing is good for you if it prevents you from exhibiting your free will. You might think for now that these things are good for you and they make you happy—but you must consider whether these things are causing you genuine happiness or whether they are simply thriving off your inferiority.

It is best to let go of the things that harm you rather than to allow them to cause more harm and cause irrevocable damage. Moreover, it is best to let go at an early stage so that you will not be too attached to it the moment you decide that it is not good for you.

Accept the Things That You Cannot Change

"Understanding is the first step to acceptance, and only with acceptance can there be recovery"

– J. K. Rowling

As much as you wish to change yourself, there are still things that you cannot do, and you must understand this in order to fully accept it. Accept the fact that you are capable of making mistakes and that you cannot solve everything, but the best that you can do is to minimize the damage brought to your life.

There are plenty of things in our lives that we cannot change, but it doesn't mean we must not do anything about it. These things may be permanent, but how we react to these things give us a completely different story.

As long as you exert your best effort to change, then that should be enough. Since there are things that we cannot change, the best thing that we can do is to embrace these things completely. See these things not as hindrances, but accept that these are important parts of life and that these are opportunities for growth.

Learn to accept the things that you cannot change so that you may not dwell on them for too long. Instead, act towards the ones that you can change, and change these things for 1) the betterment of yourself and 2) the betterment of others.

Maintain a Healthy Lifestyle

"Eat healthily, sleep well, breathe deeply, move harmoniously."

– Jean-Pierre Barral

People think that insecurity is a psychological and mental issue and that it does not involve the physical body. The truth is, it *does* involve the physical body. In whatever we do, we must not neglect the importance of the physical body because without it, we cannot function completely.

Inasmuch as insecurity is a psychological issue, the state of the physical body plays a very important part. An unhealthy lifestyle is one of the factors why one feels insecure—when you are physically unhealthy, there is also a tendency for you to be psychologically, mentally, and emotionally unstable. A healthy body results in a healthy mind, and a healthy mind produces wise and rational decisions based on fact and reason and simply not on one's emotions.

Moreover, maintaining a healthy lifestyle contributes to better self-control, especially in terms of our emotions. We cannot disagree that an unhealthy lifestyle results in imbalanced bodily processes that affect the way we function.

Being healthy is not simply being physically healthy or emotionally healthy. Being healthy is a combination of both aspects.

Work on Eliminating Your Insecurities One at a Time

"In order to move forward, you will have to stumble along the way, but every falter in your stride just makes your next step even stronger."

– Lindsay Chamberlin

Nothing worth having ever comes easy, and one cannot achieve success in a difficult task with just a single step. Remember that a big step is a combination of small, single steps, and that applies the same for eliminating your insecurities.

It is clear that you already have your goal set and that you are more than willing to achieve this goal, but you must remember that you cannot do this the easy way.

Instead of trying to eliminate your insecurities all at the same time, try working on each of them one by one, and you will see that you will be more productive at the end of the day. Moreover, it is better for you to work on fighting each insecurity one by one because it will give you more focus, and it will not confuse you with the other insecurities, most especially if these insecurities belong to different aspects of human life.

There may be a lack of shortcuts in the process of defeating your insecurities, but the long path is often paved with life lessons and notable experiences.

Develop Your Skills to Boost Your Self-Esteem

"Every man has a specific skill, whether it is discovered or not, that more readily and naturally comes to him than it would to another, and his own should be sought and polished. He excels best in his niche—originality loses its authenticity in one's efforts to obtain originality."

– Criss Jami

Insecurity often results from the thinking that you lack any skills whatsoever and that you are incapable of learning any type of skill. This is not true. Every person has different skills; it just so happens that there are common skills among people, and people are led to think that these are the only skills possible for one to attain.

You should not be limited by this line of thinking. There are endless possibilities when it comes to skill development. One way of overcoming your insecurities is building up your self-esteem, and one way of building your self-esteem is developing your skills; thus, following this logic, one way of overcoming your insecurities is through developing your skills. When you see that you also have skills, and that you are capable of these, then you will believe in yourself more, and you will cease to think that other people are better than you.

In order to achieve this, you must be willing to try a lot of new things. We have heard of the term "hidden talents," and this is true. There are times when our skills are "hiding" from us only because we have not explored enough possibilities for them to appear. Sometimes, skills hide in the weirdest of opportunities, but you must not let this weirdness hinder you from exploring these said opportunities. Who knows? Maybe your interests and skills lie in those opportunities, and that the only reason why you haven't acquired these skills is because you have been so afraid in the past.

As much as every person is unique, every person is also special and talented. We are always meant to excel in one or more things, and you are not an exception. You can do it!

Start Taking Action

"Live your truth. Express your love. Share your enthusiasm. Take action towards your dreams. Walk your talk. Dance and sing to your music. Embrace your blessings. Make today worth remembering." – Steve Maraboli

This is the last tip that will be given in this book: **take action.** Every tip in this book will be deemed useless if you do not at least try to apply them in real-life. For you to enjoy the benefits of being insecurity-free, then you must begin with the will to fight against it.

The tips provided in this book require a lot of willpower—*strong* willpower in fact. Succeeding in your task of defeating your insecurities is a long process, since we are dealing with thoughts, emotions and personal traits. Still, remember that nothing is impossible if you are really up to the challenge. Do not be afraid to start taking action. To emphasize further, there is nothing wrong in taking risks.

It all begins with a single step. Take that chance and see the difference.

How to Apply Key Ideas for the Best Results?

After presenting 25 tips on how to defeat your insecurities, this chapter shall provide a summary of each tip along with some additional suggestions:

Identify the source of your insecurities

Every time you feel that insecurity striking, grab a pen and paper and make a list. This way, you can easily identify the things that make you insecure, and you will easily know what obstacles you are supposed to overcome.

Acknowledge your fears

You can never overcome *any* fear without acknowledging it first. Admit to yourself what you are afraid of, and then work your way towards conquering these fears.

Consider your strengths

You do not have to be conceited for you to feel secure, but it helps to know your strengths so that you will not feel underestimated by other people. Think of that certain thing where you feel the warmest, and see whether this area is actually your forte.

Acknowledge your successes and achievements

When you achieve something, whether big or small, acknowledge it. There should be no achievement left unrecognized, for you must remember that you worked hard to achieve these things, whatever they may be, and you deserve to be recognized for that.

Ask friends to help you identify your best qualities

It is only you who can identify the specific people whom you trust. You know who you are honest with, and you know the people who are *not* afraid to tell you things straight to the face. Explain your situation to these people and allow them to help you.

Surround yourself with supportive people

You are aware of those who can make you feel good about yourself and those who do the exact opposite. Choose to surround yourself with those who belong to the former category, and you will see a significant change of point of view in your life.

Avoid being around people who make you feel insecure

If you really wish to cut off all the sources of your insecurity, then you must also choose to avoid being around people who bring about these insecurities. It may be difficult at first, but remember that it is better to cut them off early rather than to allow them to make you feel worse.

Socialize more

In order to boost your confidence around other people, be sociable. Do not be afraid to make friends; do not think that no one will like you as their friend. There will always be people who will be interested in what you have to say. Every person has a different story, and you will never know how much a person can change your life until you allow them in yours.

Identify what hinders you from overcoming your insecurities

Similar to identifying the sources of your insecurities, you must also identify what are the obstacles that prevent you from defeating these insecurities. What is stopping you? What is out there that is preventing you from making a move? What is preventing you from changing yourself? Ask yourself these questions first, and by answering these questions, you can come up with solutions.

Always make a reality check

Paranoia will get you nowhere. Before you choose to believe in something, make sure that there are facts to back it up. There will always be people and thoughts who will try to bring you down, but you must not allow them to succeed.

Stop comparing yourself to others

There is no need to compare yourself to others because you are a unique individual. You have your own strengths and skills, and you need not check whether you have the same skills that others possess.

Do not make your insecurities obvious

Learn to hide your insecurities so that you may avoid being perceived as weak by other people. Thinking that other people can see your insecurities will only make you feel conscious about every action, but not showing these insecurities builds up confidence.

Discuss your feelings

It is always better to discuss your feelings rather than keeping them all inside. If you cannot find someone whom you can discuss your feelings with, a journal and/or a blog is an adequate substitute.

Remember that you create your own destiny

Do not allow other people to control your life—in thoughts, in words or in action. You control your own life, and your decisions are your own, not others'.

Take risks to change your behavior

It is not easy to get rid of your insecurities. In fact, it is easier to live with them rather than eliminate them. Still, you must think long-term when it comes to major decisions in your life. Always consider the long-term benefits and not the short-term ones because it is the ones in the long run that matter the most.

Develop courage within yourself

Alongside taking risks, you must develop courage within yourself because courage is the most important virtue to possess if you want to proceed with anything. Without courage, you will not be able to do anything else. It all starts with the willpower to achieve something.

Consider the negative consequences of insecurity

Know that insecurity will get you nowhere. Remember what you are putting at risk if you decide to live with your insecurities.

Think of the positive effects of overcoming insecurity

The positive effects of overcoming insecurity may serve as your motivating force. Always keep your thoughts positive and these will translate to actions.

Always be true

In everything you do, remember to always stay true. Stay true to yourself and to others in order to make the process of defeating your insecurities worthwhile and genuine.

Learn to let go of the things that make you insecure

Do not choose to hold on to the things that make you insecure. It may be difficult as some things may be dear to you, but anything that prevents you from making decisions on your own is not good for you; thus, they must be set free.

Accept the things that you cannot change

No matter how much you wish to change your life completely, there are some things that you cannot change. Acceptance of this fact is one thing, while embracing these permanent things is another.

Maintain a healthy lifestyle

Insecurity is not restricted to the psychological and mental domains of the body. In aiming to overcome your biggest insecurities, you must also pay attention to the physical body. Remember that physical fitness translates to mental, emotional and psychological fitness.

Work on eliminating your insecurities one at a time

Nothing can be achieved in just a single step. Instead of trying to take shortcuts, take one step at a time when eliminating your insecurities. This way, you can stay more focused on your task, and you will achieve greater productivity.

Develop your skills to boost your self-esteem

Being determined to fight your insecurities is one way of helping yourself, but you must help yourself further and until the end. You know that low self-esteem is one of the biggest symptoms of insecurity, and in order to solve the bigger problem, begin with dealing with the smaller ones. Help yourself by developing your skills in order to boost your self-esteem.

Start taking action

Lastly, if you wish for these tips to take effect, then you must begin by taking action. None of these pieces of advice will translate to reality unless you do as such. Nonetheless, may these tips serve their purpose not just in theory, but more importantly, in practice.

Printed in Great Britain
by Amazon